frank lloyd wright

frank lloyd wright

Marco Dezzi Bardeschi

Hamlyn

London   New York   Sydney   Toronto

twentieth-century masters
General editors H. L. Jaffé and A. Busignani

© Copyright in the text G. C. Sansoni, Florence 1970
Photographs: Liberto Perugi and Balthazar Korab
© Copyright this edition The Hamlyn Publishing Group Limited 1972
London Sydney Toronto New York
Hamlyn House, Feltham, Middlesex, England
ISBN 0 600 39205 8

Filmset by Photoprint Plates, Rayleigh, Essex, England
Printed in Italy by: Industria Grafica L'Impronta, Scandicci, Florence
Bound in Italy by: Poligrafici il Resto del Carlino, Bologna

Distributed in the United States of America by Crown Publishers Inc.

contents

List of colour illustrations

List of black and white illustrations

The problem of Wright today

Today, ten years after his death, it is hard to write critically about the great American architect Frank Lloyd Wright. It is hard, at least, if one is trying to write not on the usual level of fulsome, conventional praise but on one where he is seen in historical perspective, and where, in a detached way, the meaning of the complex works he left behind him can be assessed.

His working life spanned more than seventy years; his activity during that time was on a titanic scale, and was always centrally important to the development and objectives of the modern movement. In his own personal development and exuberant creativity he touched areas that were probably more disparate, more far-flung in space and culture, than those of anyone else in the history of architecture. All this took place over more than three generations, and meant that the influence of his personal experiments spread in a kind of chain reaction, with incalculably wide results. A systematic bibliography of all that has been published on his work by his admirers and his detractors all over the world is almost impossible to compile; so that, even today, the extent of his influence, direct or indirect, in particular cultural areas, cannot be precisely established. This influence is something that critics of the future will have to examine; Wright's many-sided activity, and the role it has played in producing a truly modern outlook in architecture, will then be properly assessed.

It is surprising, though, to find that no one has recently sought to put him into his true position in the world, to look systematically at all the problems his work has raised. In the case of every other major architect in the modern movement this has been done. A great deal has, of course, been written about him by critics, and much can be learned by studying the work of architects he has influenced, or who have been reacting against him—in either case, these can be understood only through an understanding of his work; but his complete and organic position in the world of modern architecture has not yet been defined.

So, in spite of all that has been written and the widespread publication of pictures of his work, no one has really taken his work as a whole and dealt with his message in all its complexity and interest. Much has been written on its various phases, individually considered—in particular on the period of his Prairie Houses—but its final stages have not really been critically considered: perhaps they are too difficult for even his most open-minded critics. The attitude to problems of form, the whole iconoclastic structure of his later work, is so unusual that architects themselves have maintained an almost total silence on it.

To avoid disappointing the reader, it must be said at once that this essay is not attempting any such wide analysis. The form of this series of monographs imposes strict limitations on the author, and these appear all the narrower when one is dealing with a man as fertile and as many-sided as Wright. Besides this, a book by Carlo Cresti on the Guggenheim Museum has recently appeared, brought out by the publisher of this one. So, instead of seeking to summarise Wright's work as a whole (and without attempting to deal fully with his biography or bibliography), the book seeks to concentrate on a number of periods in his development. This may stress one or the other too much, but it is homogeneous in its attempt to find the sources of Wright's ideas by examining the enormous field of cultural and other influences upon him, which among other things allows one to realise just where he moved away from those who occasionally worked with him.

This book concentrates on the exhausting years in which he was first putting across his ideas (1889–1909); the decisive year being 1910 when Wright first published his ideas. This was the year in which he broke boldly and decisively with his own past plans and with his family.

What our generation now needs to do, therefore, is to connect the various fragments (large though these may be) and arrange them as they should be in the dazzling context of Wright's work; to evaluate what can be seen, objectively, to connect them and thus understand the scale of values that is implied in them, however much they differ from one another. In other words, the critic must be detached from the two kinds of criticism that have so far been applied to Wright. The first kind is warm and sincere but far too conventional and one-sided; it involves unquestioning admiration of the master, and really seems to be more a kind of family history than anything historically valid. The second is that of his detractors, who are repelled or simply made suspicious both by Wright's work and by what he himself says of it. Both these schools of criticism are incomplete and far too personal and subjective.

Even Wright's own autobiographical writings are only partially useful in clearing up what is difficult to interpret in his work. They have the obvious defects of having been written after the event, with hindsight and over-elaboration; in fact, they are the most suspect form of autobiographical writing – the 'reconstruction' of events at a distance, with everything slanted to suit the author's own preferences. In other words, they are more a key to Wright's own character and to his subconscious than a useful tool with which to solve the problems of his work. ·

One type of criticism concentrates on the artist himself, judging his work poetically and subjectively from the inside; ignoring all outside influences and analysing his work as if it were entirely the result of free creative impulses, meaningful in themselves and for themselves. This kind of criticism deals with each work on its own, evaluates it for itself and compares it with what came before it; in this way it seeks to make parallel the experience of the man himself and the work he produces. This seems to me to have happened in critical assessments of Wright, both those that deal with the ideas of space involved and those that deal with his forms (it is odd to find them mutually exclusive). Until now Wright's spatial ideas, based on the interpretation of his favourite term 'organic', have been most useful in showing what he really meant by the Prairie Houses or the Guggenheim Museum; but even these have tended to become too closely and exclusively concentrated on each individual work and so to become too narrow in comparison with the wide range of problems involved.

Pls. 35–39, Fig. 32

Wright knowingly took the word 'organic' from Louis Sullivan and applied it to his own work; although it had a good deal of success and became widely known, in the end it was obviously wrongly used. Giedion realised that it was impossible to avoid identifying the term organic with Wright's work, and with no one else's; indeed, that it was an outsize case of tautology. 'Wright's whole career was an endeavour to express himself in what he called "organic architecture", whatever that may be . . . When on January 25, 1940, he lectured at Jackson Hall, Boston, he devoted his entire discussion to this problem of his life. He tried by a sort of Socratic dialogue, a give-and-take between himself and his audience, to define and explain it. But his effort was futile. It was clear, finally, that no explanation was possible in words.'

This is an obvious case of the difficulty of establishing a relationship between the concept of a work, when its author tries to explain it, and its execution; his theoretical analysis is bound to be unsuccessful.

For this reason many of the critics who have written about Wright have sought to explain the formal structure of his works by comparing them with parallel works by his contemporaries in a number of parts of the world and in a number of cultures. This comparison has the obvious advantage of showing the originality of Wright's message and the way he was so clearly ahead of his contemporaries; on the other hand, in seeking to bring together and to label everything, it has often interpreted his work in an abstract and unreal way, seeking to find a unity in things that are in fact quite separate and distinct. It has also, in seeking for analogies of form, highlighted parts of Wright's work at the expense of others (we shall deal later with the actual influence of historical preconceptions of form, both oriental and nearer home, in his work).

This kind of criticism is echoed by architects in their work, when they seek to copy individual details from him before they have properly assimilated them. It often produces variations on the theme of his formal ideas, which are always fascinating; often these are good in themselves, but they are yet another example of the way in which Wright has more often been imitated than properly understood.

In Europe in particular, Wright's message has found it hard to come across, because for many years the terms 'rational' and 'organic' have been considered as standing in opposition to each other. Recently efforts have been made to interpret Wright in a rational way and to consider what he contributed in the field of technology; in other words, to see him not as a romantic escapist, but as a man in the main line of development that runs from illuminism and Jeffersonian realism to the clean formal lines of modern American technology. Works of Wright's such as the Larkin Building, the Unitarian Church at Oak Park, Falling Water, the Johnson factories, etc., which best illustrate this side of him, are cited in support of it.

Figs. 13–14
Figs. 11–12, 25–29, 31, Pls. 22–25

All this is made even more interesting by Wright's own remarkable personality and by the increasingly legendary character which the great men of the modern movement have been achieving; in Wright's case, too, by the messianic, oracular, absolute tone of what he said.

Today (one may as well admit it frankly) we are witnessing a temporary eclipse in the reputation of this great but uncomfortable man. This is because too much of his work has so far been linked with that of earlier generations, and, in spite of everything, too much of it still remains to be understood, and weighs too heavily upon contemporary studies; it does not mean that his message has been exhausted, merely that most of it still needs to be discovered or even rediscovered, and that there is a growing sense of resentment at the fact that we all owe Wright a debt which is still unpaid, and in the meantime have become weary and bewildered as we wait to pay it.

In the present atmosphere heroes are 'demythologized', if not actually debunked. The great men of the modern movement are no longer considered sacred, the movement itself is discussed in an atmosphere of perplexity and uneasiness. Either harshly or with honest embarrassment, the young realise that Wright, great innovator though he was, kept very far from the main social problems of our day and even further from those of his own; that criticism of him must in all cases remain subjective, and that anyone who comes to look at his work must first of all come up against a certain degree of narcissism in this self-regarding artist.

The time in which we live has seen the end of artistic idols and personal

Creative individuality

1 Schiller Building, Chicago, Illinois (by Adler and Sullivan, 1891–1912). Wright's first office was on the top floor

myths, and architectural studies are now determined to avoid what is rarified and sterile, to keep social problems strictly in mind, to ally themselves with advanced civil and political movements and to have some connection with the mass-media; in other words, to be truly effective and popular. In an atmosphere of this kind the creative activity of an artist like Wright can hardly fail to be suspect; for in spite of its prophetic nature (which if anything took him further than ever from the concrete everyday problems of the masses), Wright never managed to establish a convincing relationship with the man in the street, to whom, after all, his work was never addressed.

This has meant that efforts to interpret and explain his work in a sociological way (which have indeed revived the adverse criticisms of those who first censored him years ago), in the light of American society, expanding rapidly at the end of the last century; efforts to assess his contribution to the problems of the world's most important industrialised society, have been doomed to failure. And this is so in Wright's case very much more than it is in that of the other great architects of the modern movement.

From the beginning of his career Wright designed for the rich, for a wealthy bourgeoisie at the very top of its particular social scale. These people were living in a way that was directly opposed to their own back-

2–3 Wright's own house at Oak Park, Illinois, 1889. Front on to the street, children's playroom

ground – in other words, in as isolated and anti-urban a way as possible.

When Wright's career began, the industrial revolution had made the towns develop more intensively than ever before, and Chicago was ahead of other industrialised cities in making its civic centre coincide with the area of large shops, hotels and offices; among these was the Auditorium, on which Adler and Sullivan were working in the very years in which Wright was employed in their office. On the one hand, in Chicago, there were the early metal-framed sky-scrapers, designed by Le Baron Jenney, by Holabird and Roche, and by Burnham and Root: the Leiter Building, 1879; the Home Insurance Building, 1885; the second Leiter Building, the Fair Building and the Tacoma Building, 1889; the Manhattan Building, 1890; the Monadnock Building, 1891; the Masonic Temple, 1892, and, finally, a masterpiece – the Reliance Building of 1890–95. On the other were the areas of temporary, ramshackle slum houses on the outskirts of the young city that was exploding upwards. But Wright remained a stranger to the large problems of working-class, standardised, collective housing; he chose freely to study the one-family house, and this meant that he had to find a new way of life for Americans. He was rightly proud of doing so, but achieved it at an excessively rarefied level, one that was inaccessible to ordinary people and therefore outside the range of the dramatic

4 Charnley House, Chicago, Illinois, 1891. Front on to the street

conflicts that characterised the struggling everyday life of expanding towns.

Wright, in other words, designed houses for those who were his equals, isolated individuals who dreamed of escaping from the towns, which they saw as machines that destroyed the individual, and as forces of alienation. 'For Wright, the house is a refuge, a cave-like shelter into which the human animal can creep, protected from rain, wind and light,' wrote Giedion; but as such it was a means of social self-destruction, and set itself up as a fundamentally anti-urban building that, far from uniting men, divided them. His one-family houses set one another off, and took no notice of one another; they were set in the broad network of monotonous greenery near large cities, as shells to protect a patriarchal privacy, recalling the silent spaciousness of the pioneers' farms; they were containers that isolated their owners, and failed entirely to communicate with others. These houses of the rich bourgeoisie were a well-furbished microcosm that competed with the town or at any rate tended to become a substitute for it; they reflected this wealthy class's vision of an oligarchical society and satisfied the needs of the new ruling class by assuming a clear-cut scale of human relations. There was the drawing room for social calls, for games, reading, study, and the actions of everyday life; there were the servants' rooms, as well; and the space around the fireplace was the most intimate part of the house, in fact it was its inner, symbolic, evocative heart, definitely in the tradition of the pioneers.

These were some of the criticisms levelled against Wright, and there was certainly something in them, but his message cannot be reduced to such small dimensions without losing much of its meaning.

His haughty, radical exclusiveness, from the ambitious start of his career, is an intrinsic, unmistakable characteristic of his work. The proud, subjective element in it is a vital part of its structure and it would be absurd to try to censure it, worse to try to expunge it; in any case, it would be anti-historical.

It was in celebrating the creative individualism of Walt Whitman, and in the cult of the personality of Sullivan, the only two forerunners of Wright whom he officially recognised, that the arrogant self-consciousness which distinguishes his ideas and his creative activity is most noticeable. Sullivan, although only fifteen years older than Wright, was not only his admired *lieber Meister* but the ineffable artist with characteristics that expressed the supernatural – his disciples affectionately called him the *Ubermensch*. Whitman, even more than Sullivan, seemed to Wright the exceptional artist who, in celebrating himself, and his own unrepeatable, existential vitality, celebrated the whole of America; thus his own creative individualism consciously summed up in itself the collective life of his country, acting as a kind of catalyst, distilling its very essence:

I celebrate myself, and sing myself,
And what I assume you shall assume,
For every atom belonging to me as good belongs to you.

Like the poet in *Song of Myself*, the artist sets himself in the centre of the universe and from this egocentric position, by digging from within, he rediscovers people, society, and the great collective unconscious.

It is this thought, this conviction, that keeps recurring in Whitman's *Leaves of Grass*:

I dote on myself, there is that lot of me and all so luscious,
Each moment and whatever happens thrills me with joy.
I know I am deathless,
I know this orbit of mine cannot be swept by a carpenter's compass . . .
I know I am august . . .
I exist as I am, that is enough,
If no other in the world be aware I sit content,
And if each and all be aware I sit content.
One world is aware and by far the largest to me, and that is myself,
And whether I come to my own today or in ten thousand or in ten million

5 G. Blossom House, Chicago, Illinois, 1892. Front on to the street

6 A. W. Harlan House, Chicago, Illinois, 1892. Front on to the street

years,
    I can cheerfully take it now, or with equal cheerfulness I can wait.

In Wright, as in every great artist, all historical experience, all his own past and with it everything with which he came into contact as his life progressed, was melted in the crucible of his creative thought, regenerated, purged of its impurities, and returned to the primary material which is then creatively handled and reorganised. The strength with which he absorbed these things was enormous, and the change took place more at an instinctive level than through a conscious cultural action of his. Although the auto-biographical clues in his books of memoirs are very valuable (particularly those in *An Autobiography, An Organic Architecture: The Architecture of Democracy* and in *A Testament*), it is in the work he actually realised or planned, rather than in his ideologies and programmes, that the communication between the architect and others is to be found; it is on the level of concrete, working results that his message takes on a life of its own and can be understood.

The understanding, or rather the dialogue, between emitter and receiver at the decisive moment is thus concentrated once again on the end product: it is the works themselves and the presences they contain which have the final word.

Beyond convention

7 Winslow House, River Forest,
Illinois, 1893

8 Hickox House, Kankakee,
Illinois, 1900.

9 Willits House, Highland Park,
Illinois, 1902

Time did not touch Wright, as it did not touch Whitman. His thought lay outside the flux of history, beyond the contradictory excitements and everyday tensions that, through ephemeral events, create it. His ideas, his thought, his determination to discover a new level of architectural study, took place, in spite of everything, in a kind of mental limbo, free of received ideas and influences, and could be assimilated in a rhythm that was like deep breathing or regular heartbeats. In him there was no terrible struggle against time, no agitated competitive feeling towards his contemporaries; his work lay right outside and beyond the possibility of clashing with others, of meeting them in head-on collision. In spite of this, from the very beginning Wright felt entirely sure that it was his vocation to be 'leader': his own sharply exhibitionistic and probably extremely complex character was yet another form of defence that allowed him to avoid too exhausting a relationship with others.

This acted as a filter which safeguarded him and assured freedom to his totally unconventional work, both in the detail of its execution and in the matter of its cultural antecedence.

'Everyone engaged in creative work,' he wrote in *A Testament*, 'is subject to persecution by the odious comparison. Odious comparisons dog the footsteps of all creation wherever the poetic principle is involved because the inferior mind learns only by comparisons; comparisons, usually equivocal, made by selfish interests each for the other. But the superior mind learns by analyses: the study of Nature.'

It was by putting his roots down into nature, seen as the source of all experience and with the whole of history in her womb, that the meditations of Wright as a young man found their greatest nourishment and support.

Wright was fortunate not to undergo a conventional architectural training of the Beaux Arts type, like Sullivan, who was dogged by it all his life. The best architects working in American towns during the eighties had had an intense even if brief period of study in Paris. Giedion quotes a remark of Hamlin, who said: 'Around 1880 ten to fifteen Americans were always to be found in the Ecole de Paris. Teachers trained in Paris were sought in every school . . . The Ecole was the model for all our American schools in which design was taught.'

Wright's initial architectural training came through a double technical apprenticeship. In 1885, when he was seventeen, his father left the family, never to return, and the young Frank, being the eldest, had to take his place as head of the family. Under his mother's able guidance he qualified as a draughtsman; he then started working in the office of Allen D. Conover and at the same time studying as a special student in the School of Engineering at the local Madison University, of which Conover was dean. It cannot be said that this experience had any very fundamental effect on his education, nor can it have been particularly congenial; for he not only failed to attend regularly but after barely two years left Madison, Conover and the School of Engineering and took the great step of moving to nearby Chicago, which could now be considered the most advanced city in the field of architectural experiment.

'No courses in architecture were held in the university of Wisconsin,' Wright wrote. 'So, several months before I was to qualify in civil engineering in 1888, I fled to Chicago to work for a real architect. I had no wish to be an engineer.' This was the step which decided his life.

What was the cultural heritage he took with him at the age of nineteen, apart from the modest technological knowledge he picked up in his short time working and studying at Madison? He knew a little–but that little was to influence him profoundly–about the contemporary discussion in Europe on the renewal of artistic studies, having heard about it since boyhood. First of all there were the fascinating and interesting subjects dealt with by the romantics, Victor Hugo's *Notre Dame* was a most import-

European influences and the Froebel 'gifts'

ant influence and one that continued throughout his life. In the whole of his *Testament* Wright quoted Hugo with surprising frequency, and considered him as oracle, chief prophet and tutelary god of the new architecture. Beside him stood Ruskin, whose *Seven Lamps of Architecture* he had probably read when he was very young, since his maternal aunts had given him a copy of it, probably at his mother's suggestion. This theoretical basis had a popularising tone about it and encouraged a critical approach; later, while he was working at Silsbee's in Chicago, Wright went over to more practical reading and copied about a hundred drawings from Owen Jones's *Grammar of Ornament*, and at the same time studied Viollet le Duc's monumental *Dictionnaire Raisonné,* an inexhaustible sourcebook of neo-medieval ideas for all the Beaux Arts architects.

Wright's grandfather, Richard Lloyd-Jones, was a Welshman who arrived in Wisconsin about 1850, with seven children. From her parents, Wright's mother had inherited a confident, gay and aggressive character that was typical of the pioneers. She took as her motto the significant words: 'Truth against the world', and with her pride and energy organised her son's progress from the moment of his birth: 'She was determined that her son should be a great builder, and she was convinced that she could predestine him to that end. Secure in her faith that her first-born would be male, she hung engravings of English cathedrals on the walls of the room which his crib was to occupy. From the day of his birth she never ceased to concentrate her willpower and her ingenuity upon fortifying that architectural ambience which had been established pre-natally.'

Apart from her, and from Sullivan (whom Wright recognised as giving him decisive moral and idealistic support) it is hard to pinpoint the exact influences during his extremely rapid progress in architecture. His first revolutionary house, Charnley House, appeared in 1890, but his own house actually belongs to the previous year, when he was barely twenty. His mother, however, must have the credit for providing him with an ingenious form of architectural training that was to be his deepest experience, and the first, irreplaceable experiment in assemblage: that is, the Froebel toys which he played with enthusiastically from the age of seven.

In both his *Autobiography* and in his *Testament* Wright mentions his debt to Froebel, and thus gives us a clue to the interpretation of the origins and the development of his ability to create from an early and complete possession of the fundamental laws of design. In 1876, his parents went from Boston to Philadelphia to see the great exhibition at Fairmount Park celebrating the centenary of the Declaration of Independence. It was here that his mother discovered the revolutionary idea tried out by Froebel and his colleagues in the Kindergartens: 'Mother's intense interest in the Froebel system was awakened at the Philadelphia Centennial, 1876. In the Frederich Froebel Kindergarten exhibit there, mother found the "Gifts". And gifts they were. Along with the gifts was the system, as a basis for design and the elementary geometry behind all natural birth of Form.' What were these gifts?

'The strips of coloured paper, glazed and matt, remarkably soft brilliant colours. Now came the geometric by-play of these charming checkered colour combinations . . . the smooth shapely maple blocks with which to build, the sense of which never afterwards leaves the fingers: so *form* became *feeling* . . . Smooth, triangular shapes, white-backed, and edges, cut in rhomboids, with which to make designs on the flat table top. What shapes they made naturally if you would only let them! . . . That early kindergarten experience with the straight line; the flat plane; the square; the triangle; the circle! If I wanted more, the square modified by the triangle gave the hexagon–the circle modified by the straight line would give the octagon. Adding thickness, getting sculpture thereby, the square became the cube, the triangle the tetrahedron, the circle the sphere. These primary forms and figures were the secret of all effects . . . which were ever got into

10 Fricke House, Oak Park, Illinois, 1902

11–12 Unitarian Church, Oak Park, Illinois, 1906. Interior

the architecture of the world.'

Thus, in Wright's education, empirical experience and the direct knowledge of materials, of elementary forms and the laws that governed them, were more important than indirect, filtered, historical experience. By playing with these toys in an embryonic unconscious but effective series of experiments on natural formal structures, Wright became able to penetrate the rhythmic structure in nature, the geometry hidden under an incoherent appearance (the cosmic geometric elements), and the games imperceptively changed into basic experience: 'The smooth cardboard triangles and maplewood blocks were most important. All are in my fingers to this day.'

Another interest of Wright's can be traced back to these Froebel toys: his enthusiasm for a system of symbolic significant values that seemed to him to assume the fundamental, archetypal forms present, even if only at a subconscious level, in all his works: 'In outline the square was significant of integrity; the circle—infinity; the triangle—aspiration; with all of which to design significant new forms. In the third dimension, the smooth maple blocks became the cubes, the square and the tetrahedron; all mine to "play" with.'

Wright always attributed a decisive importance to the learning activities of the nursery school, and, when he looked back on his own experience with the Froebel toys, which clearly, although unconsciously so, took place at an enthusiastic, vocational level, he must have been influenced by Sullivan whose lecture on first principles had the significant title of *Kindergarten Chats,* and was in the form of a dialogue between the teacher and an imaginary pupil.

13–14 Administrative building of the Larkin Company, Buffalo, New York, 1904. Exterior and interior

We have seen how Whitman's exalted egocentricity was the model for Wright's own. From his earliest days Wright had known that what he was to do would be entirely radical, but Wright was radical, as Whitman was, because of his unshakeable belief in his own absolute and prophetic powers. From the start (Charnley House, and his own home at Oak Park), Wright quite explicitly showed that he meant to reject all preconceived ideas, everything that had been used before; that he intended to proceed from within himself, relying on his own powers and using the truth he had discovered through direct experience in an entirely subjective way.

A new dimension in nature

Whitman's message found a wholehearted response in the young architect. Whitman was a passionate, full-hearted singer, the incarnation of all the young primordial energy of America advancing with faith and confidence to annexe unknown lands in the name of democracy. And it was the same great stretches of countryside, the same sounds and smells and distances, that Wright assimilated and, between 1895 and 1909, interpreted in his architectural work with his own unique, personal and prophetic vision.

Both men rejected the academic ideas and standards of their day, and for the same reasons. Both put their trust in the individual and in his personal initiative, both felt a profound affinity with nature, both mistrusted all forms of intellectualism ('a morning glory at my window satisfies me more than the metaphysics of books', Whitman wrote) and of secondhand culture. Wright's non-style corresponds exactly with Whitman's, which embarrassed and bewildered the critics of his own day. Both artists were indifferent to 'decoration' in itself, both sought to use the language of spontaneous, everyday speech, indeed of slang, in order to arrive at what was most essential and authentic; and both looked for analogies of an almost biological kind in their efforts to get beneath the surface of problems and to penetrate what was essentially important in them. All this led the two men into a revolutionary use of what was most primitive, most deep-set, in the American tradition. Whitman celebrated the land in epic form, and Wright's ideas for new ways of living matched them; both were directly influenced by the spirit of the pioneers.

The Chicago School

Against this cultural background, what were the specifically architectural influences on the 'young heretic' in the exciting atmosphere of Chicago in the eighties? In his *Testament* Wright deals interestingly in what was happening in American architecture in 1888. 'Among the architects practising in America when I entered Adler and Sullivan's offices,' he wrote, 'Richardson had the high honour of the field; Beaux Arts graduate, Bostonian, well-connected with the better elements of society . . . Eventually he became the most productive and successful of those men, the great eclectics of the time. Many of them fell in love with his love of the Romanesque.

15 Martin House, Buffalo, New York, 1904

16–17 A. Coonley House, Riverside, Illinois, 1908. Exterior and interior

Yes, his Romanesque soon amounted to something wherever his fellow architects were concerned with a style.' It was neo-Romanesque, still romantic in background but sober and clearcut in quality; and it undoubtedly influenced Sullivan, who, in 1886, after Richardson's death at an early age, clearly appeared to accept the task of carrying on where Richardson had left off. But in spite of all that Richardson had done to found a new architectural system based on essentials, there was something in him that worried Wright: an excessive preoccupation with historical tradition that appeared in all his work, a bent that was openly European and a result of his Beaux Arts training. For this reason, although he admired Richardson as both man and artist, Wright substantially rejected his work and projects ('a powerful romantic eclectic. Gone now').

Then there were the revivalists, who dug back into history in all kinds of ways, all of which cancelled one another out. Wright ridiculed their ragbag methods, and the way they raised false, superficial problems; their ideas, he felt, deserved nothing more than oblivion. 'McKim, Mead and White, Richardson's élite running competition, were also Beaux Arts men', he wrote. 'Their eclecticism was of another more elegant order, faithful to the more choice effects of early Italian Renaissance. In their affected, cultivated stride they took the ancient buildings verbatim. Whenever they found the buildings they admired, they copied them, enlarging the details by lantern slides. Used them straight . . . Gone now . . . Richard M. Hunt, darling of New York's four hundred, head of their procession of Fifth and other American Avenues, was a good technician with a finished preference for the French-Gothic ensemble . . . Gone now.'

Finally there was the group which consisted of Adler and Sullivan, Major Jenney, Daniel H. Burnham and John Root, Cass Gilbert, Van Brunt and Howe, of them, Wright wrote, 'the only men indicating genius above engineering capacity and the capabilities of front men were Louis Sullivan and John Root.'

As far as European culture was concerned, it weighed lightly, as we have seen, on the young Wright. He always seemed suspicious of everything that came from a place that was culturally so distant and came to America by indirect ways; but it was the culture his mother's parents had left behind them and we know, too, that what was going on in Europe was noted with interest in Chicago and that Wright himself was well aware of the awakening in matters of art there–both theoretically and in practice. 'As premonition, then, the pre-Raphaelites had appeared in England but they seemed sentimentalist reformers. Beside the mark. Good William Morris and John Ruskin were much in evidence in Chicago intellectual circles at the time. The Macintoshes of Scotland; restless European protestants also–Van de Velde of Belgium, Berlage of Holland, Adolph Loos and Otto Wagner of Vienna: all were genuine protestants but then seen and heard only in Europe.'

All in all, Wright seemed to feel that what was happening in Europe was too remote to have any relevance to the American scene. He felt that it was on the sidelines, both because the past weighed too heavily upon it, and because it was too remote; Van de Velde's journey to America was the only point of contact. 'Came Van de Velde with Art Nouveau, himself predecessor of the subsequent Bauhaus. Later, in 1910 when I went to Germany by instigation of Professor Kuno Franke, there I found only the rebellious Secession in full swing. I met no architects.'

These quotations from Wright's autobiographical works show how proudly and forcefully he repudiated any suggestion that his own early work might be compared with what was being done at the same time in Europe. But historically this attitude is untenable and it is now up to new critics to examine how Europe and America interacted in those years–how each influenced the other, and what the relationships and exchanges between them were.

Adler, Sullivan and Richardson

In his early years, however, Wright was deeply impressed by Adler and Sullivan. Adler was the elder and the more experienced, and Wright admired his businesslike spirit, his ability to organise, his confident grasp of technology, his rational, practical outlook. Sullivan he admired as a man with a great future ahead of him, a brilliant artist with an outstanding mind, gifted with both creative power and the capacity to reason. Here was a man who could go beyond the limits of convention and what was known as common sense. 'But more important than all,' Wright wrote, 'a great protestant, grey army engineer, Dankmar Adler, builder and philosopher, together with his young partner, a genius, rebel from the Beaux Arts of Paris, Louis H. Sullivan, were practising architecture there in Chicago,

about 1887.' They were 'the only moderns in architecture . . . with whom, for that reason, I wanted to work.'

Wright may have ungenerously relegated Richardson among the revivalists (though at the head of them), but in fact his influence on the architects of what was known as the Chicago School was undoubtedly of decisive importance as a source of inspiration to Wright both now and later.

It was Giedion who pointed out the affinities between Berlage and Richardson. Both turned to history, indeed used it in their work; but they used it in so critical a way that there was nothing at all nostalgic about it, no lingering and loitering over earlier forms. What they used were bare, simplified structures, skeletal forms that called themselves Romanesque, the

23 Imperial Hotel, Tokyo, 1916–22. View of the exterior

basic element of whose composition was the wall as a flat surface, without any additional ornament, simply a 'plane' which goes back to its original function – that of being both a generator and a container of space. Berlage's example had a decisive influence in Europe. 'Above all we should show the naked wall in all its sleek beauty', he wrote in 1905, in *Gedaken über Stil in der Bankunst*, referring to his Amsterdam Stock Exchange. He was also the first European advocate and admirer of Wright's work, at the time of the Wasmuth publication on it in Berlin, after George E. Elmslee, Sullivan's new partner, had invited him to the United States in 1911. Giedion recalls that it was through an article in the *Schweizerische Bauzeitung* in 1912, an extensive résumé by Berlage himself of a lecture he had given in Zürich that Le Corbusier first came to know Wright's work. But it should not be forgotten that Richardson had come to many of the same conclusions as Berlage a good deal earlier, and that his Sever Hall in Boston, built as early as 1878, showed how the weight of the historical past could be sloughed off, and a pure, level surface achieved.

The lieber Meister

In 1887, then, Wright was eighteen, and went to work as a draughtsman in Sullivan's office for twenty-five dollars a week. His *lieber Meister* was then only thirty-one; between 1886 and 1889 he was working on the Auditorium Building which passed through many stages and, as was the case with Richardson's buildings, gradually achieved greater freedom of form, greater coherence and a stricter, more pared-down composition.

Sullivan had studied in Paris from 1874 to 1876, and in 1879 had gone to work for Adler, whose partner he became in 1881. Their partnership lasted until 1895, and their final separation was the result of a profound crisis in Sullivan's life, one from which he never recovered; to this crisis, Wright appears to have contributed decisively.

It was the restrictive, conventional Parisian education, rejected but never entirely thrown off by Sullivan, however hard he tried to escape it, that Wright was referring to when he made a famous lighthearted remark in 1896. Given the tempting chance of being sent to Paris or Rome at the expense of Daniel Burnham, Wright said frankly that he had already had quite enough of them through Sullivan, who had 'helped to ruin the Beaux Arts for me or me for the Beaux Arts'.

But quite apart from any glib remarks of the kind, Richardson's Marshal Field Wholesale Store in Chicago quite clearly influenced Sullivan in his work on the Walker Building of 1888–89, and shows how an advanced idea passed straight from Richardson through Sullivan and on to Wright. All this influence was on the practical level, and Wright had plenty of opportunity to be formed by it; but there were also Sullivan's theoretical ideas, which had a really decisive influence on the way Wright's work developed. These were the central years of Sullivan's activity as an architect, during which he developed his highly original idea of architecture as an organic creative process, a cognitive act that shaped and arranged human activity, freeing it from all the conventional relationships that had always crippled it.

Sullivan was undoubtedly the most dramatic figure in America in the eighties, eager to clear the air and to forge new critical tools, and always opposed by the monolithic power of the academic architects. In his book *Kindergarten Chats*, which appeared in 1901, Sullivan tried to define what he meant by 'organic' architecture, clearing the field first of all and analysing what the term could not define, could not contain within itself. The definitive result of his thinking appeared only in 1924, the year of his death, under the title of *An Autobiography of an Idea*, and this shows without any doubt at all the important role Sullivan's ideas played in the formation of Wright's theories.

We know, too, how Sullivan's generous efforts were tragically doomed to failure, just when the Chicago School was about to break through and conquer its opponents, whether monumentalists or revivalists; for in 1893 came the 'ugly business' of the Chicago World Fair, coinciding with Wright's first independence in a studio of his own. 'When I put the gold letters Frank Lloyd Wright, Architect on the plate glass panel of my office door in "The Schiller", in 1893, the causes of the cultural lag I encountered lay in the social bias created by the growing eclecticisms of the practices of the A.I.A. Dead Sea fruit of inadequate architectural education. The true character of American life was being submerged.' The heroic group of young men gathered around Wright had already seemed threatened; now they were suddenly overwhelmed by what he called the disaster of the World Fair. Until then Chicago had been a cradle of new ideas and experiments, but after the World Fair eclecticism and classicism triumphed. The Fair, Wright said, was a 'tragic travesty–florid countenance of theoretical Beaux Arts formalisms; perversion of what modern building we had then achieved by negation; already a blight upon our progress. A senseless reversion.'

But above all: 'Owing to this first World's Fair, recognition of organic American architecture would have to wait at least another half century'; for the change of direction which followed was a violent one, a case of general inebriation: 'The ambitious ignoramus in the architectural profession throughout America was captivated.'

Undoubtedly, however, there were advantages even in this disaster. It encouraged the neo-medievalists and neo-classicists into really euphoric extremes, and they produced any number of formalised designs, some of them on a remarkable scale; occasionally these were real masterpieces of escapism, like the neo-Gothic Woolworth Building in New York, 1911–13. But it also produced the kind of stormy decisive action that appears in Wright's autobiographical writings, it strengthened his fighting spirit and made his objectives seem very much clearer. In other words, it increased the intransigence of his own attitudes to architecture.

The World Fair brought things to a head. Wright's basic problem was how to reconcile a revolutionary originality with a levelling, flattening

'Truth against the world'

25

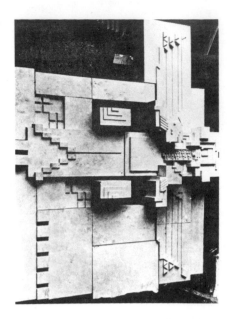

24 F. C. Bogk House,
Milwaukee, Wisconsin, 1916.
Panel carved in stone

routine of work that was safe and unadventurous; how to bring to it an alternative system believed in with such conviction that it could not be reduced or circumscribed; how to back his own idea of truth against convention, conformity and compromise. For Wright, the years 1893–95 were decisive. His group of friends and colleagues gradually fell apart and in the end he felt alone; yet he was deeply persuaded that his message was authentic, that he really had a new system of original values ('truth against the world').

So, in the first years when he was working on his own in his office in the Schiller Building, the original group known as The Eighteen was gradually disbanding; because, as Wright put it, 'all were friendly but not willing to cut the umbilical cord to the Colonial or the French château, to the English manor house or the grandomania of Beaux Arts days.' Gamble Rogers was lost to the virtuosity of the Gothic, Howard Shaw to the English Colonial. Wright himself might have succumbed: he had great facility as a designer, a lively imagination and an enviable capacity to absorb every kind of style, a quality that allowed him to steep himself instinctively, and always with great originality, in every kind of formalised historical material. (There were, for instance, the drawings he took when interviewed by Sullivan: 'I took the onion-skin tracing of ornamental details I had made from Owen Jones, mostly Gothic, and made them over into "Sullivanesque". Or there were the romantic, flowery decorations he did for Silsbee.) The temptation to opt for what was rich and exuberant must have been great; had he done so, he would with little effort have become a part, indeed a brilliantly successful part of the fashionable world of drawing-room architecture. But the World Fair, and the sight of what was advanced in architecture giving way before it, had a very different effect on Wright from its effect on Sullivan. Sullivan was plunged by it into a paralysing dismay, and felt certain that the battle was quite definitely lost. Wright, on the other hand, felt that the World Fair was the last straw; the final proof that the system was worn out, and that the only radical alternative was to be found in a conscious rejection of all the imported 'history' that destroyed it, and a return to a human, harmonious and balanced relationship with nature.

Instead of the powerful, absurd, self-defeating code based on these historical styles brought in from outside, a new code must be found, based on a naturalness that was not brought in from outside; one that was an intrinsic part of American life, that worked well, that was biologically human or – in Wright's term – organic. The escapism of Morris, the formal experiments of Art Nouveau, which were then so influential in the West, were not a part of American life. Wright already saw his way clearly to the Prairie Houses: 'But, now independent, I didn't use the fascinating ornament, had struck out a new line in a field of my own – the American dwelling: the nature of materials and steel intention', he wrote. 'Of what was going on abroad at this time I had no knowledge nor any interest in. Nor was there any Japanese architectural influence, as may be seen in these illustrations.'

We shall return later to what Wright says (in the last part of the piece quoted here) about these apparent external influences. But for the present we must see what he did in developing his ideas, as he himself said, in the one-family house.

Wright had gone to work for Silsbee without special enthusiasm, and had stayed with him for less than a year (as compared with the two he had spent with Conover in Madison). Silsbee had at that time a great deal of work designing dwelling houses in the current fashion. This meant the late Victorian enthusiasm for revivalism, which had gone from the picturesque tradition of the Queen Anne style to the Shingle style, which has recently been much discussed. 'Silsbee could draw with amazing ease', wrote Wright. 'He drew with soft, deep black pencil strokes and he would make remarkable free-hand sketches of that type of dwelling peculiarly his own at the time. His superior talent for design had made him respected in Chicago. His work was a picturesque combination of gable, turret and hip with broad porches quietly domestic and gracefully picturesque. A contrast to the awkward stupidities and brutalities of the period, elsewhere.'

At Silsbee's office, then, Wright had for the first time come across a contemporary architecture that was anything but conventional and academic, and that was applied, at a fairly high level, to the intelligent interpretation of the housing needs of well-to-do American families, to the most efficient and functional way of using the land available for their houses, and to establishing a proper relationship between them and their surroundings. It was in these very efforts of Silsbee's that we can find the germ of the idea of a house centrifugally placed to face out towards nature. In his *Frank Lloyd Wright: the first golden age*, Grant C. Manson writes: 'In the guise of the oriel and the bay came the idea of continuous fenestration and the centrifugal plan; from the English porch grew the spacious American verandah, spreading the house upon its site and giving it low, informal lines; the translation of the English pantile for siding into the old Colonial grey shingle and the flowing contours it suggested such as the eyebrow dormer and the bell-shaped cupola; bold, fanciful chimneys, moulded brickwork, plastic ornament in terracotta and carved wood. Despite its puzzlements, the net result in America of the vogue for the Queen Anne was an adaptable, elastic kind of domestic and related architecture that was better perhaps suited for living on the North American continent than any style which had preceded it.'

But there is no doubt that it was Wright's five years in Adler and Sullivan's office that allowed him to study the individual house, and to do so with increasing autonomy as time went by; for Sullivan considered it beneath him to deal with it, and concentrated on more ambitious, large-scale buildings, leaving more and more responsibility for the private houses they built to Wright. This led to the episode which brought the final break between them – Wright's acceptance of unofficial jobs, out of office hours and carried on at home; for his growing family meant that he needed the money he could earn in this way.

Wright had married early, in 1889, and had immediately set to to build a house for himself; like his other buildings of the period, it embodied the ideas he had been considering. It was built on a small piece of land at Oak Park, a suburb of Chicago later to become famous for Wright's houses in it; at that time it stood eight miles west of Chicago, a place full of greenery and on the edge of open country. Silsbee's influence is obvious in Wright's own house, particularly in the projecting bow-windows and the very steeply pitched roof; and in his use of the large shell-shaped fireplace, considered as the heart and centre of the house, Wright was openly in the American tradition. Giedion pointed this out by showing, for comparison, the plan of a country house by G. E. Woodward published in 1873; this is in the form of a cross, the arms of which contain the rooms used for every-day life (hall, parlour, library, dining room, with kitchen and service rooms); while the point at which these all meet consists of a monumental fireplace. Memories of the Shingle style are also evident in Wright's own house, as Scully has shown; indeed, he found an example of a prototype house built at exactly that time, the designs for which Wright very likely saw published. The plan of the house, too, shows, if only timidly, Wright's idea of space as a single unit, in which life was lived in a unified way, instead of being divided into single separate compartments.

From then onwards, Wright concentrated on the dwelling house. As is well known, he disliked the idea of the dwelling house being considered in vertical units: to him the skyscraper was merely a 'mechanical device'

The house at Oak Park

to 'multiply the land area as many times as possible and sell it over and over again', and from the start it was clear to him that speculative building of the kind was quite contrary to his basic ideas of organic architecture, which planned a building as a balanced part of its site, and in horizontal, not vertical, terms. What Wright himself wrote about his early houses is illuminating: 'The human figure appeared to me, about 1893 or earlier, as the true *human* scale of architecture . . . The quiet, intuitional, horizontal line (it will always be the line of human tenure on this earth) was thus humanly interpreted and suited to modern machine performance.'

The idea of the dwelling house

Wright's message, which brought him international acclaim in 1910, was derived from his ideas on the dwelling house, which he had considered in a completely new way. British architects had been working on the problem since the 1860s, but if one compares Wright's ideas with theirs, (especially with those of Mackintosh), it is entirely to his advantage. Like Wright, they were seeking to reform the living unit from the inside, to free it from the conformity of centuries in which it had simply stuck in its academic groove, and to bring alternative ideas to it. But they sought to do this by making fundamental changes in the interior arrangements of the house, that is, in the mere detail of what was used in it. Mossir and his associates concentrated entirely on the decoration and furniture and sought to give a new function to traditional craftsmanship. They concentrated on objects in everyday use, and tried to 'train' people's eyes—that is, to persuade them to use a style that had some meaning, some cultural purpose, some eloquence through association; but in doing so they barely touched on the problems of the interior space of the house (except as something that was important for its associations or something homogeneous, to be lived in), or its planning and distribution (positivistic functionalism was barely considered, in those days).

Wright, on the other hand, was the first architect to consider essentials. He too began in a way that could be called introspective, he too worked

from the inside of the house and sought to renew it. But he managed to overcome the centuries-old division of the house into separate, artificial sections, box-like rooms that in no way communicated with one another, to break down the silence and exclusiveness of this kind of plan and to make the interior space of the house into a single flowing unit in which the various activities that take place in a house could be developed. This in no way meant that he neglected the details of furniture and decoration. On the contrary, the influence of Sullivan on his ideas for the interior arrangement of the house was so strong, even in the years of his maturity, that later critics have felt it places him unfailingly in the 19th century, where his work began.

But it was not only the interior of the house that Wright considered; he went outside it, linking it wherever possible with the exterior, with nature and reality and life out of doors; and so for the first time a conscious effort was made to set the building suitably in its surroundings, to break down the traditional barriers that divide the inner and outer life of the house. The outer walls were opened up for continuous windows.

Wright's ideas on the organic reconstruction of the dwelling house thus recovered its fundamental links with the land around it. A biological unity was achieved between landscape and interior living space, which allowed the two to be joyfully united. The inner life of the house was to participate in the life of nature and to find, once again, its role as an integral part of the countryside. The site thus became an inalienable part of the architectural plan, quite apart from any passing limitations that might be imposed upon it by property divisions and by the capitalist method of developing suburban areas into separate building lots.

In the last years of the 19th century an idea of the kind could stand up only in a country like America, which was free enough of the past which weighed so heavily upon Europe – where, in any case, architecture seemed to become progressively more and more bound up with fragmentary urban life. American life at the time was still attractively close to the spirit of the 'frontiersmen', an exuberant spirit that was colonising new areas in its own way, without too much historical influence pressing upon it and with the

27–29 E. J. Kauffmann House
(Falling Water), Bear Run,
Pennsylvania, 1936. Details
of the exterior and interior

influence of nature still powerful. All this was within the framework of
democratic ideas and of the 'commonsense' teachings of Emerson, Whitman,
Cooper, Greenhough and Thoreau.

Thoreau preached a return to the land, and implied a hatred of the city,
seen as a great productive machine, not as a place to live in. Wright felt
this even when he was working with Sullivan: 'There, in Adler and Sullivan's office,' he wrote, 'high on the tower of the Auditorium in Chicago,
I worked for nearly seven years, with George Elmslie beside me; and sometimes I looked out over Richardson's romantic arches, down to lake
Michigan; or, very often, when it was dark, I looked down at the enormous,

Bessemer Steel Works that reddened the night sky, down to Chicago South. I looked from those high arches over the enormous city that was growing down below, while the trams of Illinois Central puffed along the lakeside.'

While Sullivan sought to solve the difficult problem of office buildings, and the great monumental issues raised by urban business life, Wright was following a more attractive idea; that of the anarchical dream of a free society of individuals. From the business life of Chicago he looked out to the green fields nearby, in which he planned houses in which man and nature would live together in a new, restorative harmony. 'To him, the city was evil incarnate,' wrote Peter Blake, 'and an evil that was growing at enormous speed. When Wright was born, the population of the United States was only thirty-eight million; when he died, it was nearly a hundred and eighty million. When he was born, less than a quarter of all Americans lived in towns; when he died, almost three-quarters had moved to the big cities. But Wright was part of the minority that stayed put; and after his death in April 1959, he was buried at Spring Green in Wisconsin, about ten miles from the place where he had been born ninety years before. It would seem that it had become a matter of principle to him never really to have left his birth place.'

Pl. 12, 13, Fig. 18   Wright's progress to Robie House, which ends his first period of single houses (rightly called by Manson 'the first golden age'), was of course a gradual one, and his plans slowly became clearer and simpler. Indeed it is possible to follow how his ideas developed in plan, structure and detail, for the houses themselves contain perfectly clear examples of Wright's changes in method and ideas.

Charnley House

Fig. 4

Charnley House (1891) was Wright's first masterpiece; he designed it while he was still working for Adler and Sullivan, but in his own time, at home. In it, the plan was simplified in a completely revolutionary way; Richardson's influence was no longer in evidence, and, in spite of its symbolic ideas, it seemed to anticipate the modern movement. Wright seemed to be expressing his belief in the essentials of form, in the need to dispense with all cloying reminders of the past. Its shape was compact and boxlike, strictly symmetrical in front with the central storey slightly pushed back and an enormous jutting loggia beneath it. The windows were simply holes cut into the compact surface of the outer wall, which was made of small Roman bricks. Wright was well aware that Charnley House foreshadowed rationalist architecture in a remarkable way: 'it is the first modern building,' he wrote: but far more important was the fact that he was also well aware that getting rid of the past, seeking essentials, indeed the whole radical spirit, was not enough to alter the nature of a building, still less to revolutionise the way of life of those who lived in it, if the architect was merely seeking a new means of expression in it. The outlook of a very young architect in his first building is, after all, generous and far-reaching. What Wright realised quite clearly even in those early days was the actual limitations of rationalism; instead of a temporary objective, it tends to turn into a definite standard, then into a cliché cloaking works that basically have little to do with it. In an argument with Loos and Le Corbusier, he once said: 'I've built a box myself', meaning Charnley House; and he meant that style in itself could not bring about a substantial revolution in living, whether the style tended to exalt and accelerate it, as happened with Morris and Art Nouveau, or to freeze and castrate it, as happened with rationalism. It must include spatial ideas within itself, it must be part of the wish to arrange space in new ways. This was why Wright considered Charnley House as a provocative manifesto, one that showed a new and revolutionary style, one that was pure and anti-Victorian; yet really no more than a simple Froebel game in solid geometry. 'The Charnley house, for all its innovation and portents, has one glaring fault', wrote Grant C. Manson. 'It is closed, hard, impermeable.

31 Johnson Building, Racine, 1936–39. Detail of the exterior

The idea of interpenetration of atmosphere and structure had not yet crystallised in Wright's imagination.'

Another exercise in solid geometry was Sullivan's residence (the Albert Sullivan House on Lake Avenue), on which Wright worked at the same time, in 1891. In it, if we omit Sullivan's own additions (the exuberant decoration on the coping, the bow-window and the fanlight in the hall, which Elmslie said were made to Sullivan's design), the essential, asymmetrical composition of the front, the steps at the front entrance, the way in which the slightly polygonal bow-window is placed to correspond with a shaded loggia divided into three, on the ground floor, the cubist geometry, all anticipate and confirm what Wright was saying in Charnley House.

The collaboration between Wright and Sullivan can and should be further examined and illuminated, in spite of valuable studies already available (Manson, Condit, Hitchcock). There is, for instance, the case of the Schiller Building, which Wright claimed to have a part in. 'Thanks to Sullivan's affection for his house in the South, it [the Schiller Building] was entrusted

Fig. 1

mainly to me, rather than anyone else', Wright wrote. There was also the embarrassing business of the Transportation Building at the Chicago World Fair in 1893. The exuberant decoration with which its walls seemed encrusted, and the overtly oriental flavour of these, may recall Sullivan's fascination with India (which also appears in his writings), but it is surprising if one considers the desire for clean formal lines so clearly shown by Wright in his first buildings. The fact is that the self-defeating decorative euphoria that appears in the Transportation Building can be considered only as the result of a need to clash head-on with the academic formalists, at their own level. Although it finally defeats the rational intention of the building as a whole, it does take on a new, intentionally unfashionable, meaning, as Peter Blake has observed, not in seeking to debase the historical, academic attitudes but in seeking an alternative by claiming a completely naturalistic and organic feeling: thus, the ornamentation became symbolic, although it was still used in opposition to the eclectic architects. 'In the eyes of Sullivan and his young assistant', wrote Peter Blake, 'symbolic images of nature began increasingly to represent images of America and democracy. America was space and landscape; Europe was city life, crowded and formalistic . . . The ornamentation of the Transportation Building was a symbol of honesty, of loyalty to the land.'

The influence of Japanese architecture

Wright found the World Fair of 1893 decisively important for another reason: because it gave him his first direct contact with Japanese architecture. Manson says that Wright first came to know oriental objects at Silsbee's suburban house at Edgewater, where he had a remarkable collection of them, but it was at the Fair that he had his first chance of considering at leisure the characteristics of a small Japanese temple, the Ho-o-den, which the Japanese government had built on Wooded Isle, a small island in an artificial lake, reached by an attractive little bridge.

In those years, in England and France, exotic objects were already very fashionable. The American painter Whistler and the de Goncourt brothers, dealers and critics, had done much to spread interest in the collection of objects from the Far East, and Japanese influence in America was already felt in the generation of McKim, Mead, and White; since the Centennial exhibition at Philadelphia in 1876, where Mrs Wright discovered the Froebel gifts that were to influence her son's development so much. Japanese objects, however, did not really widen the artistic horizons of the rich; they became a refined, exotic, affected form of escapism. But with Wright it was quite otherwise: the sight of this Japanese temple was a revelation. It might be the dreariest academic copy of a building on which the past weighed too heavily, but it came to him at the very moment in which he was seeking new means of expression, and it suggested riches to him. The plan of the Katsura temple was symmetrical but flexible, with angular pilasters along both the exterior and the interior (where they formed a central, more emphatic frame); and between them the space was a single harmonious whole, in which, as if by some ritual magic, but quite without outside pressures, all traditional partitions and inner dividing walls had vanished and the whole building turned on the 'tokonoma', the reliquary that, as the centre of the ceremonies there, was the centre of contemplation and of the cult of the home. All this Wright felt for the first time, and the meaning of the plan, at once rational and symbolic, struck him profoundly, fascinating him. 'The plan of any Japanese house is a study in higher mathematics,' he was to say in 1905, on his first visit to Japan. But it was not only the plan of the temple, with all that was formally absolute about it, and the patient centuries of training that had brought it to where it was that impressed Wright: technically and stylistically it proved extremely important to him as well. In the Ho-o-den the outer partitions that divided the space used for life within from the outside were simple sliding screens on the inside, and transparent or translucent panels carrying continuous windows mounted on wheels and therefore sliding as well. Only a fifth of the outside wall was fixed, and this was the back wall which protected the building against the wind. The central hall and the side tea rooms were therefore open spaces, communicating completely with the garden and the delightful natural world outside. As far as its structural characteristics were concerned, Wright must have been struck by the clarity with which the contrast between the bearing parts of the building, and the parts it bore, was shown: the bearing parts consisted of clearly shown supports of black wood, enclosing white panels. The roof jutted out very far, giving ample strips of shade, and this horizontal spirit was entirely in line with the idea Wright tried out in his Prairie Houses.

All this meant that in spite of its disadvantages, the Chicago World Fair was decisively important to Wright, who just at that time was setting up in his own office where he was developing and working on his own projects.

It is well known that Wright insisted on the importance of what he had learnt from Japanese architecture; and there is no doubt, as many observers have remarked (Berlage himself in 1925; also Hitchcock, Manson and Blake), that without having seen for himself an actual example of that architecture, however modest and misleading it may have been, the decisive revolution in his style and attitude during the early years of work would not have been possible. 'During the time I worked at Oak Park,' he wrote in *An Auto-biography*, 'the elimination of what was superfluous, the artistic process of simplification in which I had been involved since I was twenty-three, found its parallel in the prints . . . I found that Japanese art had a truly organic character, that it was closer to the earth, that it was a more direct product of the primary condition of life and labour and therefore closer to the modern – as I saw it – than the European civilisations, alive or dead.'

Winslow House, which belongs to the same year, 1893, is in fact the first proof that Wright had deeply assimilated what to many would have been a mere momentary experience. (Frankly, the Ho-o-den shown at the Chicago Fair, if photographs are anything to go by, today must make us smile rather than excited, so crude, so modest and so ingenuous is it compared with the real oriental buildings it parodied.) In Winslow House, the rectangular plan is broken on the two shorter sides by an extension to the living room, still in the Shingle Style, on the one hand, and the large *porte-cochère* on the other; and it is divided by a central axis on which the main fireplace is built, occupying the exact heart of the house. The greatest innovation, however, is the hip roof, which juts out low at the height of the architrave of the windows on the upper floor, overhanging the lower part of the house to an unusual depth. This way of raising the roof from a shadowed first floor, which is treated as a continuous, single, horizontal strip, makes this a completely new work in which the clean, compact surfaces of the outer walls in dark orange Roman brick cling continuously but strictly to the superb natural landscape in which it is set.

Opposite the entrance, Winslow House has a remarkable example of pure blocks of various geometrical shapes assembled in a way that recalls the Froebel gifts. The relationship between the continuous semi-cylindrical windows of the ground floor and the polygonal framework of the staircase seems to foreshadow motifs which would later be used by the middle European neo-plastic movement. But the arrangement of the roofs is still the most striking thing about it – their steepness, their carefully calculated shapes, their wide projections and the vigorous play of shadow which enriches them. This is also true of the nearby stables, which contain something Wright was fond of – a tree growing through the roof itself.

Winslow House, in spite of a plan that is still rigid, is the first link in the chain of Prairie Houses that show Wright's amazing lucidity in planning, and his creative fertility. Their innovations, both structural and stylistic, were so important that even today their message is still significant and surprising.

Wright's ideas tested in practice

In all that he achieved between 1892 and 1909, Wright experimented so widely that it is hard to pick upon any one building as an example of a particular moment, or of a particular radical choice. It would appear that he planned as he breathed, all day and every day, and needed to absorb and digest the most disparate elements; indeed, this early work of his is an exuberant cauldron of them, often contradicting one another in the same building, which makes it hard to find unity in it. Wright seems to have tried out every kind of style, and made every kind of experiment, before finally deciding that a particular element (if that was the case) had no future in it and was unproductive; and each one of us naturally looks for what to him seems most interesting, significant and fertile in them. There is, in fact, a kind of criticism that considers Wright in order to 're-use' what he was saying in other buildings, whether actual or on paper, and if this is done then it would seem a mistake to dismiss (as his traditional detractors have done) even the houses he designed secretly while working for Sullivan, which express the often brutal difficulties he had in dealing with clients, and show his first wholesome, dramatic collision with an immoveable reality. This collision strengthened and recharged his ideas of what he was to do.

In spite of this unyielding obstinacy, Wright from the first seems to have had no intention of playing the part of the unshakeable, abstract theorist, the misunderstood prophet, or the victim frustrated by a reality untouched by higher things. On the contrary, he sought first of all to put his theories into practice, to try out and test his ideas; if even a single one of his plans failed to become reality he considered it a painful setback. In other words, he seems to have measured his own success, his own capacity to have an effect on reality and to defeat the prevailing system, entirely by the concrete results obtained, on each occasion, on the building site. Even those known as the 'bootlegged' houses, ten of which were planned and nine built, apart from a few really incredible cases which no one would suspect of being his (but which Wright himself may have considered as examples of how low a man must sink in order to survive), gave him a chance to make experiments, perhaps without the client even realising what he was doing, within the

Fig. 6   limitations allowed him. This is so particularly so in the Harlan and McArthur houses, and even more so in the house he built for Walter Gale.

In the early days, indeed, Wright sometimes showed a curious willingness to use traditional forms and historical styles. No doubt he had clients who would have liked him to build them a medieval castle, and he seems to have taken their wishes rather too seriously. This was something that was never to happen again so openly, ingenuously and thoughtlessly, except perhaps

Pls. 14–16, Figs. 21–23   in the single case of the Imperial Hotel in Tokyo. It is surprising to see the Palladian Blossom House, built in the neo-Colonial style of New England, or the Ionic columns of Bagley House (1894), which was also in the Colonial style, but this time the Dutch, taken from the kind of building Silsbee liked (see his Jamieson House, 1889); or again the unfortunate neo-Romanesque Municiple Boathouse on Lake Mendota, which was the result of a competition won in 1893. Then there is a house Wright designed for one of his earliest clients, W. Nathan Moore, which seems like a direct, if intelligent, neo-medieval building in the Tudor style, with the traditional wooden

Fig. 7   supports and details to match in period style. Even Winslow House, which has grown well away from all this, has some surprising little decorated columns and arches near the fireplace; and finally there are the fronts of the four terraced Roloson Houses, the single example in Wright's work of terraced houses on a traditional plan in which historical touches are happily

32 Guggenheim Museum, New York, 1943–58. Detail of the interior   combined with an organic geometrical arrangement of squared blocks, under high English-style roofs.

The Prairie Houses

Luckily Wright soon, and permanently, shrugged off these traditional styles and continued on the way he had begun with Charnley House and Winslow

House. In 1895 came his plan for a multi-storeyed office block for the American Luxfer Prism Company, the first prophetic example of a prismatic skyscraper in glass and concrete, and an authentic even if still crude 'curtain wall' that pre-dates the modern movement by more than twenty years. The profit he made from this building gave him the chance to build himself a new office beside his own house at Oak Park; and the interior developed his revolutionary use of space as a single, vital element.

Pl. 3 In this studio of his Wright tested his ideas on the use of space, and everything in its interior – visual effects, careful variations in the arrangement of walls and ceilings – was used to achieve a flowing, unified effect. At the same time, the use of a continuous horizontal strip at the height of the architraves of the doors (corresponding to Le Corbusier's measurement of a man's height with his arm raised) is an effective way of giving the various interior spaces a unity by imposing a human dimension upon them.

This studio was the first building to put Sullivan's organic ideas into practice, although it did not really escape the pitfalls inherent in these ideas. A modest building like the Romeo and Juliet Windmill (1896), on the other hand, shows Wright for the first time using elementary geometrical forms, which can still be traced back to the Froebel ideas, together, and it is interesting to see how they foreshadow the particular way in which he was to assemble varied forms of the kind in his mature years. In the slightly rhetorical but effective octagon which he used in those years to contain the autonomous studies and libraries of the house, a rhomboid-shaped wedge was set, formed of two triangles joined at the base. Thus he had, at one and the same time, a central polyhedron as the basic, static structure, with a dynamic form that generated tensions in opposition to it.

Out of all Wright's enormous output during these years, it seems interesting to point out two houses planned but unfortunately not built, and given with full detail in Wright's book published by Wasmuth in 1910. These are McAfee House and Devin House, and what is most interesting about them is the way in which the octagonal form of the library and the long rectangular living room consist of box-like geometrical forms set at an angle of 45°, thus producing two abutments.

As the Prairie Houses were planned, Wright came more and more to alter the static Silsbee-type bow windows, which at first (in his house at Oak Pl. 1, Figs. 2–3 Park, for instance) were merely attractive parts of the front. Gradually they took on a more important centrifugal position in the outside wall, and came to appear as arrows or dynamic points, vectors that gave an energetic continuity to the exterior, which enclosed the living space within. As the years went by, this became clearer, more persuasive and more deliberate. Figs. 4, 7 Charnley House and Winslow House show the first timid signs: simple 'swellings' appear in the outer wall, showing, along the sides of the house, that specific areas for daily living exist (living room or dining room). The layout of the houses became longer and thinner, and then, from the end of the century (Heller House in 1897 and Husser House in 1899), the sense of straining outwards became greater and they escaped from the basic rectangular plan. Sometimes this was achieved through having a side entrance, as in the plan for the Ladies' Home Journal (1901), which gave a kind of official send-off to the Prairie Houses (*A home in a Prairie Town* was in fact the title it was given by the magazine); sometimes through a still traditional reception room like the one in Harley Bradley House (1900); sometimes through extra space for service rooms, as in the complex Dana House of Pl. 6–7 1904. In Heurtley House these ideas reach a point at which they provide a definite optical climax, heavily windowed and, as far as possible, following an underlying right-angled grid, at 45° to the main axis, which follows the hips of the roof, actually reproducing them in the living room. This is taken Fig. 9 a stage further in Willits House, where the long main body of the house ends in pairs of opposing crosslines at the very points of tension and escape towards the garden, in the dining room and reception room; large porches emphasise this outward thrust.

The wedge-shaped additions which until then had shown that Wright was firmly convinced his houses should be stretched out on the landscape, thus emphasising their horizontal character ('in this prolonged horizontal line,' he wrote, 'I see the true horizon of human life, I see the symbol of liberty'), suddenly disappeared in the early years of the new century; his method of designing seems to have been reconsidered, and then to have continued in a rational way, moving in a single direction—that is, a classical one, squarely based on the angle of 90°. The directional emphasis seems to have been replaced by compact U-shaped blocks, or else by enormous hollow rectangular pilasters, as in Barton House and Wright's two best-known buildings from this period, the Larkin Building in Buffalo and the Unitarian Church at Oak Park. In this way Wright seems to be seeking to recover a centripetal harmony that is substantially classical.

The extensions to the main outline, arrow-like breaks in the axis, reappear in Wright's final period of research on the Prairie Houses; they have now become definite terminal features, shown effectively in the Tennis Club at River Forest, and finally in the design which synthesised this whole process—Robie House, the most original and forceful of all Wright's houses for the unity and conviction with which he carried through his ideas. Like the Tennis Club, Robie House has an absolutely uncluttered plan. In order to avoid making it a part of the main building, the service area is set asymmetrically against one end of it. Because of this, the main body of the building consists of a single living area, the living room-dining room on the first floor, and the playroom on the ground floor; the pivot of this living area is the fireplace and the staircase, which link the two floors. Robie House shows all the essential elements developed by Wright over a period of twenty years: a solid, unifying main block, the plan of which is very long and rectangular; the main weight of the building concentrated on wide rectangular pilasters at the corners; continuous windows on the outer wall, made harmonious by rhythmically arranged frames; the short ends finished in con-

33 Beth Sholem Synagogue, Philadelphia, Pennsylvania, 1954. Detail of the roof

Figs. 11–14, Pl. 9

Pls. 12, 13, Fig. 18

trasting arrow-like projections; a wide porch at each end, protecting a large area in the living room; and above all (a characteristic element, which emphasises the unified life beneath it) a steep, heavily eaved roof, with its hips dynamically angled, broken only at its most central part by the brickwork of the chimney, which is the heart of the house and the nub of the whole building; finally, an interior that has entirely got away from what is eclectic and commercial, with the furniture and decoration both moveable and built in, considered as part of the architect's responsibility in providing a unified way of life within the house; in the case of Robie House, it is built on a system of horizontal strips and vertical lines; the horizontal being those of the functional elements in the house, and of the ceilings, the vertical being those that carry the floors and ceilings, and the vertical parts of the furniture itself (table legs, chair backs, etc). As in the Larkin Building and the Unitarian Church at Oak Park, the resulting use of the interior space of the building foreshadows cubism and neo-plasticism.

Figs. 13, 14
Pl. 9, Figs. 11, 12

At this point it may be useful to consider just who Wright's clients were, as a recent study by Leonard K. Eaton has done. They were men directly involved in the rapid industrialisation of the country, men who, through their initiative and nothing more, had reached the very top of the social ladder. Some of the richest of these were businessmen, bankers, middlemen of all kinds, sons of rich tradesmen both retail and wholesale, men dealing in insurance and property, but rarely professional men (they include three lawyers) or scientists (three physicists). Essentially they were self-made, and this seems significant for it means men who, unlike those with a traditional way of life, were open to new aesthetic adventures; in other words new men ready to go beyond the conventional and fashionable way of life and to find some new and original form of it. So Wright, acting on and through these clients, chose what was probably the only way to achieve his own revolution in living habits and in architecture; by working from above, from the top of this young oligarchical class, rather than from the bottom of it. The main reason for Wright's success in Europe from 1910 onwards lay, therefore, in the overwhelming authenticity of his message, which did not depend merely on an idea or on some ideological programme, but drew its strength and its conviction from concrete examples, from buildings that already existed.

This attempt to find the sources of Wright's early work, until 1910, has not been an end in itself; rather, it is a necessary task if the real meaning of his many-sided and exuberant work is to be seen in a new perspective, beyond the myths that have attached themselves to Wright as a person, and if a new generation is to consider and appreciate him. Zevi was right in comparing the present climate of uncertainty with that of the first decade of the century, so tellingly described by Mies van der Rohe. In today's atmosphere, in which heroes are toppled and myths reconsidered, it is certainly not the memory of Wright as a personality that is going to show us the way ahead. Yet his personal life does teach us a remarkable lesson. This is that the act of designing is something in which everything in the artist is concluded and synthesised; it is the result of a long process, and what comes through, whether we like it or not, and whatever subtle conclusions may be drawn from it, is merely the distillation of the artist's own self, the message he had to pass on to us. Like every other interpreter, the architect is, in the final analysis, faced with himself; and he must wonder how well he has managed to deal with the problems of his own society at that particular moment—problems that grow progressively more complex and more difficult, indeed may become unanswerable. As Whitman wrote: 'Do I contradict myself?—very well, I do contradict myself (I am large: I contain multitudes).' It is by drawing upon broad, far-reaching ideas of the kind that critics must interpret Wright, as every great artist is interpreted, for the generations ahead.

2

4 - 5

6

8

9

10

12

14

16

17

18

19-20

21

23

26

27

30

31

33

35-36

37

38

42

43

44

Description of colour plates

1 Wright's own house, 428 Forest Avenue, Oak Park, Illinois, 1889

2 House of Nathan G. Moore, Forest Avenue, Oak Park, Illinois, 1895. Present condition

3 Wright's Studio, 951 Chicago Avenue, Oak Park, Illinois, 1895

4–5 House of Frank Thomas, 210 Forest Avenue, Oak Park, Illinois, 1901

6 House of Arthur Heurtley, 318 Forest Avenue, Oak Park, Illinois, 1902. Front on to the street.

7 House of Arthur Heurtley, 318 Forest Avenue, Oak Park, Illinois, 1902. Front on to the garden.

8 Hillside Home School, Hillside, Spring Green, Wisconsin, 1902

9 Unitarian Church, Oak Park, Illinois, 1906

10 House of P. A. Beachy, 238 Forest Avenue, Oak Park, Illinois, 1906

11 House of Dr G. C. Stockman, Oak Park, Illinois, 1908

12 House of Frederick C. Robie, 5757 Woodlawn Avenue, Chicago, Illinois, 1909

13 House of Frederick C. Robie, 5757 Woodlawn Avenue, Chicago, Illinois, 1909

14 Imperial Hotel, Tokyo (now destroyed), 1916–22

15 Imperial Hotel, Tokyo (now destroyed), 1916–22

16 Imperial Hotel, Tokyo (now destroyed), 1916–22

17 'Hollyhock House', Sunset and Hollywood Boulevards, Edgemont Street and Vermont Avenue, Los Angeles, California, 1920

18 House of Charles Ennis, 2607 Glendower Road, Los Angeles, California, 1924. Detail

19–20 House of Charles Ennis, 2607 Glendower Road, Los Angeles, California, 1924

21 House of Charles Ennis, 2607 Glendower Road, Los Angeles, California, 1924

22 House of Edgar J. Kaufmann or Falling Water, Bear Run, Pennsylvania, 1936

23 Building of the administrative offices of S. C. Johnson & Son, 1525 Howe Street, Racine, Wisconsin, 1936–39

24 Building of the administrative offices of S. C. Johnson & Son, 1525 Howe Street, Racine, Wisconsin, 1936–39

25 Building of the administrative offices of S. C. Johnson & Son, 1525 Howe Street, Racine, Wisconsin, 1936–39

26 House of Herbert F. Johnson, Wind Point, north of Racine, Wisconsin, 1937

27 House of Herbert F. Johnson, Wind Point, north of Racine, Wisconsin, 1937

28 House of Paul R. Hanna, 727 Coronado Street, Palo Alto, California, 1937

29 Taliesin West, Maricopa Mesa, Paradise Valley, near Phoenix, Arizona, 1938

30 Taliesin West, Maricopa Mesa, Paradise Valley, near Phoenix, Arizona, 1938

31 Taliesin West, Maricopa Mesa, Paradise Valley, near Phoenix, Arizona, 1938

32 Taliesin West, Maricopa Mesa, Paradise Valley, near Phoenix, Arizona, 1938

33 House of Stanley Rosenbaum, Riverview Drive, Florence, Alabama, 1939

34 House of Gregor Affleck, Bloomfield Hills, Michigan, 1941

35–36 Solomon R. Guggenheim Museum, New York City, 1943–58

37 Solomon R. Guggenheim Museum, New York City, 1943–58

38 Solomon R. Guggenheim Museum, New York City, 1943–58

39 Solomon R. Guggenheim Museum, New York City, 1943–58

40 Price Tower, Bartlesville, Oklahoma, 1953–56

41 Beth Sholem Synagogue, Philadelphia, Pennsylvania, 1954

42 Greek orthodox church, Milwaukee, Wisconsin, 1956

43 Greek orthodox church, Milwaukee, Wisconsin, 1956

44 Kalita Humphrey's Theater, Dallas, Texas, 1959

Biographical outline

Frank Lloyd Wright was born at Richland Center, Wisconsin, on June 8th, 1869. His father was a clergyman, William Russell Cary Wright; his mother Anna's maiden name was Lloyd-Jones. Soon after his birth the family moved to Weymouth, Massachusetts, and stayed there until 1877. It was at the exhibition celebrating the centenary of Independence at Philadelphia in 1876 that his mother discovered the Froebel 'gifts' which gave the young Frank his first lessons in design.

About 1879 the family returned to Wisconsin—to Madison, where Frank went to the Second Ward School. In 1883, his father left the family, never to reappear, and Frank began training as a draughtsman in the office of Allen D. Conover, dean of the local school of Engineering, which he joined as a special student. In the spring of 1887 he left the university and went to Chicago, where he worked for Lyman Silsbee, came across the Shingle style, and started designing for his maternal uncles and aunts. At the end of 1887 he worked, for a few weeks only, in the office of Minard L. Beers, then went on to work for Adler and Sullivan, with whom he had a five-year contract from 1889. From then on, he considered Louis Sullivan his *lieber Meister*.

In the same year, 1889, he married Catherine Tobin and built his own house at Oak Park, a village eight miles from Chicago, soon to become famous for his buildings there.

While working for Sullivan he began to accept work in secret; ten houses were planned, and nine built. At last, in the spring of 1893, Sullivan discovered this; the break between them was abruptly made, and Wright gave up his job.

The Chicago World Fair had enormously encouraged the taste for classical and monumental architecture when Wright started working on his own. Between 1893 and 1909 he worked in Chicago –from 1893 to 1896 on the top floor of the Schiller Building in Randolph Street, and after that in a studio which he built for himself beside his own house at Oak Park, which in the meantime had been enlarged. He was able to do this thanks to the multi-storey office building he designed for the American Luxfer Prism Company, a design that may be called the prototype curtain wall façade.

A remarkable amount of work passed through his studio at this period. As a rule, this consisted of country houses or isolated dwellings, and his clients were always wealthy.

In 1905 Wright visited Japan. He had already become enthusiastic about Eastern architecture through his discovery of Japanese prints and through the replica of the Katsura temple he had seen at the World Fair in 1893, and his visit to Japan confirmed him in this enthusiasm. From then onwards, ideas from the East became more and more apparent in his work.

His private life had altered, meantime. In 1904 he had built a house for a client named Chaney, and in the years that followed fell in love with Mrs Chaney. In the autumn of 1909, the pair left their respective families for a long visit to Europe, first to Berlin to prepare the Wasmuth edition of Wright's book, then to Florence, where they spent more than a year. It was a decisive step for Wright to take: for the first time he left America, where he had been idolised, and stayed away until 1911, while the newspapers carried on a campaign against him. 'I thought I would shelter in Florence with the woman who was then involved with me through rebelliousness and love', he wrote. When he returned to America he chose Spring Green, Wisconsin, as the site for his home and studio, and began building a house there: it was the first Taliesin.

There, on the 'splendid hill' (Taliesin East), he began to design again, but, although his fame abroad made him the best known architect of his day, he had few clients. His most impressive work of the period is Midway Gardens, of 1914, which has a strongly oriental flavour. But this period of phantasy and escapism was ended by a sudden tragedy: a Negro servant went mad, killed seven people at Taliesin and set fire to the building. The dead were Mrs Chaney, her two children and four of Wright's young assistants.

The press took the event as a moral judgement on Wright, who, with his extraordinary will-power, managed somehow to survive the blow.

He was encouraged to continue by being offered a prestigious piece of work–the Imperial Hotel in Tokyo. So, between 1915 and 1921, he worked on this fantastic project, a kind of fairytale palace full of local influences. Wright's prestige stood higher than ever when the building survived the terrible Tokyo earthquake of 1923, but his personal life was once more tragically marred. Miriam Noel, a sculptress he lived with and eventually married, proved to have a serious mental illness that took her to an asylum and finally to her death, after her divorce from Wright in 1927.

During the twenties, Wright turned in yet another direction for inspiration; this time, to the Maya temples at Chichen Itza in Yucatan, Mexico. Here, perhaps, he found traces of a certain primitive and authentic American tradition; and in his plan for the Tahoe Summer Colony, in California, in 1922, the formal influence of certain Indian buildings was also evident.

In the early twenties, in California, Wright also experimented with cement block houses (Millard House, Pasadena, in 1923; Storer House, Los Angeles, 1923, Charles Ennis House, Los Angeles, 1924). In 1924 came another tragic event, his studio at Taliesin was burnt and with it all his most precious documents and drawings. 'During this terrible destruction', Wright wrote, 'a crowd of people stood on the hill, their faces lit by the flames . . . and some of them jeered at the madman who declared that Taliesin would rise again, after all that had happened there.' But Taliesin was rebuilt, although for a time Wright was deeply in debt and much harrassed by legal prosecutions. By this time he was living with another woman, the Montenegrin Olga Lazovich (Olgivanna), who until very recently kept the keys of Taliesin, which were recently handed over to Wright's son and Svetlana Stalin.

About the same time Wright made a number of plans for multi-storey office buildings including, in 1924, the National Life Insurance Company's skyscraper. He also made a project for a skyscraper with residential towers for St Mark's-in-the-Bouwerie, New York City (which was to be used only twenty-five years later: see St Mark's Tower (the Price Tower) Bartlesville).

With the slump in 1929, Wright's work decreased, as commissions dwindled. His reply to the Depression was to turn his studio into a Foundation, in 1932, where architectural students could study his work in progress at Taliesin.

At the same time he began to involve himself again in the public discussion of cultural matters. His most recent work was shown first at the Chicago Art Institute, and later, in 1932, at the important exhibition of contemporary architecture at the Museum of Modern Art in New York; here, though, he was distressed to find himself in the company of Le Corbusier, Mies van der Rohe, and the younger European architects.

This indirect contact with the younger generation did not prove sterile for Wright, however, for it made him reconsider the meaning of his work as a whole. Until then it had gone forward in an episodic, fragmentary way, but from 1934 onwards, he sought to give it a satisfactory framework, and, with his young pupils at the Foundation, began work on a series of studies for a model town, Broadacre City, planned to extend horizontally across its site, with an acre of land allotted to each family. This was the American reply to Le Corbusier's intensive, rational Ville Radieuse, in which distances were overcome by the use of new science-fictional means of transport. Some of Wright's best theoretical writing has been spent on this subject: in *The Disappearing City* (1932), *When a Democracy builds* (1945), *Genius and the mobocracy* (1949) and *The Living City* (1958). Broadacre City was the town exploding into the open country, in opposition to the alienating concentration of metropolitan life, and discovering a balance with nature that was both new and very old.

34 Frank Lloyd Wright

One of Wright's most successful buildings in the thirties was Falling Water at Bear Run, Pennsylvania; a house that did more than any other to win round public opinion, and that was in no way out of line with what European architects of the modern movement were thinking. In it Wright showed, however, not so much that he had been converted to rationalism as that he had enriched his own ideas through contact with those of the rationalists.

This was Wright's second golden age. Apart from Falling Water, he built the Johnson Administrative Building at Racine, Wisconsin, and the much admired winter quarters of the Foundation (Taliesin West) in Paradise Valley in the Arizona Desert. 'Taliesin West looks out over the edge of the world . . . magnificent, indescribable in words.'

He also brought his original Prairie Houses up to date in bare, essential forms; in Hanna House (1937) and Rosenbaum House (1939).

In 1937 Wright visited Russia, and published his impressions in the October, 1937 number of the 'Architectural Record', under the title of *Architecture and Life in the U.S.S.R.* In 1939 he gave a series of lectures at the Royal Institute of British Architects in London, published under the title of *An Organic Architecture: the Architecture of Democracy.*

Wright was now intent upon the use and assembling of curved units: the plan of the Johnson Building was based on a circular model. In the houses for Herbert Jacobs, Gerald Loeb and V. C. Morris, and in the project for the Elizabeth Arden Resort Hotel at Phoenix, Arizona, this idea of the curve progressively moved away from the plan to take in a third dimension. 'The reality of a container lies in the space which it contains', Wright was fond of saying, paraphrasing Lao-tse, and he was now seeking to synthesise the demands of the horizontal spread of nature and an original idea of the inhabited space. It was the spiral line, as an intrinsic, dynamic and organic part of the building, that now fascinated him. He had made a single—and ingenious—effort to deal with the idea in his project for the Gordon Strong Planetarium at Sugar Loaf Mountain, Maryland, in 1925; but now he returned to it with more conviction, trying to make an embryonic prototype, a kind of small model of a helicoid space; the V. C. Morris shop in San Francisco, 1948.

But it was only with his plans for the Guggenheim Museum, that these creative ideas of Wright's really reached maturity. In it he sought, and managed, to achieve a singleness of purpose and result that had a profound effect upon the idea of interdisciplinary studies and communications.

The same theme was developed in his plans for a multi-storey garage at Pittsburgh in 1947 and in the extraordinary projects for Greater Baghdad, made for King Feisal II of Iraq in 1957, buildings which were to have stood on an island in the river Tigris and were to have included an emblematic spiral in glass and gold (a reference to Aladdin's lamp). Wright's final work upon matters of form thus ended in exuberant but unfulfilled and basically empty projects.

Among his works after the Second World War were the Unitarian Church at Madison in 1947, and the Florida Southern College at Lakeland, Florida, which took from 1938 to 1959; the eighteen-storey tower at Bartlesville for the H. C. Price Company, completed in 1956; the project for the Civic Centre at Madison on Lake Monona in 1955; the plan for a bridge across San Francisco Bay in 1949; the plan for a Mile-high Building (Mile-high Illinois) on the shore of Lake Michigan in 1957; a project for the Arizona State Capital, 'Oasis', Phoenix, Arizona, in 1957; and finally a project for the Civic Centre of Marin County in California, in 1959, built after his death.

In 1949 Wright was given the gold medal of the American Institute of Architects and 1951 important exhibitions of his work were held in Zürich and Florence.

In 1953 he was given the gold medal of the National Institute of Arts and Letters in America, and at the same time his project for the Masieri Memorial on the Grand Canal in Venice aroused great opposition, and was finally blocked, in spite of widespread support from the enlightened, by bureaucratic ideas and local inertia.

Wright died in Phoenix, Arizona, on April 9th, 1959 and is buried at Spring Green. His remains will be taken to Taliesin.

35 Frank Lloyd Wright at his drawing board

Chronological list of works and projects

1887 Participation in the project for All Souls Church for Jenkin Lloyd-Jones. *Projects:* The Misses Lloyd Jones house, Helena Valley, Spring Green, Wisconsin. Unitarian Chapel, Sioux City, Iowa.

1888 Drawings shown to Sullivan and Adler when applying for a job *Project:* Falkernan Houses, Chicago, Illinois.

1889 Frank Lloyd Wright house, 428 Forest Avenue, Oak Park, Illinois. Perforated screen, dining room ceiling, Oak Park Studio, Chicago, Illinois. Glass ceiling light, Oak Park Studio, Chicago, Illinois.

1890 James Charnley house, Ocean Springs, Mississipi. Louis H. Sullivan house, servants' cottage and stables, Ocean Springs, Mississipi. *Projects:* Henry N. Cooper house and stables, La Grange, Illinois. W. S. MacHarg house, 4632 Beacon Avenue, Chicago, Illinois.

1891 James Charnley house, 1365 Astor Street, Chicago, Illinois. Albert W. Sullivan house, 4575 Lake Avenue, Chicago, Illinois.

1892 George Blossom house, 4858 Kenwood Avenue, Chicago, Illinois. Robert G. Emmond house, 109 South Eighth Avenue, La Grange, Illinois. Thomas H. Gale house, 1019 Chicago Avenue, Oak Park, Illinois. Dr Allison W. Harlan house, 4414 Greenwood Avenue, Chicago, Illinois. Warren McArthur house and stables, 4852 Kenwood Avenue, Chicago, Illinois. R. P. Parker house, 1027 Chicago Avenue, Oak Park, Illinois. Victoria Hotel, Chicago Heights, Illinois.

1893 Walter Gale house, 1031 Chicago Avenue, Oak Park, Illinois. Meyer Building, 307 West Van Buren Street, Chicago, Illinois. Municipal Boathouse, Carrol Street, at Lake Mendota, Madison, Wisconsin. William H. Winslow house and stables, Auvergne Place, River Forest, Illinois. *Project:* Library and Museum competition, Milwaukee, Wisconsin.

1894 Frederick Bagley house, 101 County Line Road, Hinsdale, Illinois. Dr H. W. Bassett remodelled house, 125 South Oak Park Avenue, Oak Park, Illinois. Peter Goan house, 108 South Eighth Avenue, La Grange, Illinois. Robert W. Roloson houses, 3213-3219 Calumet Avenue, Chicago, Illinois. Francis Woolley house, 1030 Superior Street, Oak Park, Illinois. *Projects:* Orrin S. Goan house, La Grange, Illinois. A. C. McAfee house, on Lake Michigan, Chicago, Illinois.

1895 Francis Apartments for Terre Haute Trust Company. 4304 Forestville Avenue, Chicago, Illinois. Francisco Terrace for Edward C. Waller, 253-257 Francisco Avenue, Chicago, Illinois. Nathan G. Moore house and stables, 329 Forest Avenue, Oak Park, Illinois. Edward C. Waller apartments, 2840-2858 West Walnut Street, Chicago, Illinois. Chauncey L. Williams house, 520 Edgewood Place, River Forest, Illinois. Frank Lloyd Wright Studio, 951 Chicago Avenue, Oak Park, Illinois. H. P. Young alterations, 334 North Kenilworth Avenue, Oak Park, Illinois. *Projects:* Jesse Baldwin house. Luxfer Prism Company skyscraper. Wolf Lake Amusement Park for Warren McArthur, on Wolf Lake, Illinois.

1896 H. C. Goodrich house, 534 North East Avenue, Oak Park, Illinois. The Misses Lloyd Jones windmill, Romeo and Juliet, Hillside, Spring Green, Wisconsin. Charles E. Roberts (remodelled interiors), 321 North Euclid Avenue, Oak Park, Illinois. Charles E. Roberts stables, 317 North Euclid Avenue, Oak Park, Illinois. *Projects:* Mrs David Devin house, on Lake Michigan, Chicago, Illinois. Robert Perkins apartment house, West Monroe Street, Chicago, Illinois.

1897 George Furbeck house, 223 North Euclid Avenue, Oak Park, Illinois. Isidore Heller house and stables, 5132 Woodlawn Avenue, Chicago, Illinois. Henry Wallis boathouse, South Shore Road, Delavan Lake, Wisconsin. Rollin Furbeck house, 515 Fair Oaks Avenue, Oak Park, Illinois. River Forest Golf Club, Bonnie Brae Avenue, River Forest, Illinois. *Project:* All Souls Building, Oakwood Boulevard at Langley Avenue, Chicago, Illinois.

1898 George W. Smith house, 404 Home Avenue, Oak Park, Illinois. *Project:* Mozart Garden for David Meyer, State Street at 55th Street, Chicago, Illinois.

1899 Joseph W. Husser house, 180 Buena Avenue, Chicago, Illinois. Edward C. Waller remodelled hall and dining room, Auvergne Place, River Forest, Illinois. *Projects:* Cheltenham Beach for Norman B. Ream and Edward C. Waller, 75th to 70th streets on the Lake, Chicago, Illinois. Robert Eckart house, River Forest, Illinois. Edward C. Waller house, River Forest, Illinois.

1900 William Adams house, 19326 South Pleasant Avenue, Chicago, Illinois. B. Harley Bradle house and stables, Glenlloyd, 701 South Harrison Avenue, Kankakee, Illinois. S. A. Foster house and stables, 12147 Harvard Avenue, Chicago, Illinois. Warren Hickox house, 687 South Harrison Avenue, Kankakee, Illinois. E. H. Pitkin house, Sapper Island, near Kensington Point, Desbarats, Ontario, Canada. Henry Wallis (H. Goodsmith) house, South Shore Road, Delavan Lake,

1901 E. Arthur Davenport house, 550 Ashland Avenue, River Forest, Illinois. E. R. Hills remodelled house, 313 Forest Avenue, Oak Park, Illinois. Fred B. Jones house, Boathouse, gate-lodge and barn, 'Penwern', South Shore Road, Delavan Lake, Wisconsin. F. B. Henderson house, 301 South Kenilworth Avenue, Elmhurst, Illinois. Robert M. Lamp cottage, Governor's Island, Lake Mendota, Wisconsin. River Forest Golf Club additions, Bonnie Brae Avenue, River Forest, Illinois. Frank Thomas house, 210 Forest Avenue, Oak Park, Illinois. Universal Portland Cement Co. Pavilion, Pan-American Exposition, Buffalo, New York. Edward C. Waller gateway, stables and gardener's cottage, Auvergne Place, River Forest, Illinois. Henry Wallis remodelled gate-lodge, South Shore Road, Delavan Lake, Wisconsin. T. E. Wilder stables, Elmhurst, Illinois. *Projects:* Lexington Terrace for Edward C. Waller, Lexington Street, Spaulding Avenue, Polk Street and Homan Avenue, Chicago, Illinois. Abraham Lincoln Center, Oakwood Boulevard and Langley Avenue, Chicago, Illinois. 'A village bank in cast concrete'. Henry Wallis house, Delavan Lake, Wisconsin.

1902 William G. Fricke house, 540 Fair Oaks Avenue, Oak Park, Illinois. George E. Gerts double house, Birch Brook, Whitehall, Michigan. Walter Gerts house, Birch Brook, Whitehall, Michigan. Arthur Heurtley house, 318 Forest Avenue, Oak Park, Illinois. Arthur Heurtley remodelled house, Les Cheneaux Club, Marquette Island, Michigan. The Misses Lloyd Jones Hillside Home School, Hillside, Spring Green, Wisconsin. Charles S. Ross house, South Shore Road, Delavan Lake, Wisconsin. George W. Spencer house, South Shore Road, Delavan Lake, Wisconsin. Ward W. Willitts house, and gardener's cottage, 715 South Sheridan Road, Highland Park, Illinois. *Projects:* Delavan Lake Yacht Club, Delavan Lake, Wisconsin. Victor Metzger house, Desbarats, Ontario, Canada. John A. Mosher house. Yahara Boat Club, Lake Mendota, Madison, Wisconsin. Edward C. Waller house, Charlevoix, Michigan. Fred B. Jones house 'Penwern', South Shore Road, Delavan Lake, Wisconsin. Ward W. Willitts house, 1445 Sheridan Road, Highland Park, Illinois.

1903 George Barton house, 118 Summit Avenue, Buffalo, New York. Susan Lawrence Dana house, East Lawrence Avenue, at 4th Street, Springfield, Illinois. W. H. Freeman house, Hinsdale, Illinois. Francis W. Little house and stables, 603 Moss Avenue, Peoria, Illinois. W. E. Martin house, 636 North East Avenue, Oak Park, Illinois. Scoville Park fountain, Lake Street, Oak Park, Illinois. J. J. Walser Jr house, 42 North Central Avenue, Chicago, Illinois. *Projects:* Robert M. Lamp house, Madison, Wisconsin. Chicago and North Western Railway station, Oak Park, Illinois. Charles E. Roberts quadruple block plan, Chicago, Fair Oaks, Superior and Ogden Avenues, Oak Park, Illinois. Edward C. Waller house, Charlevoix, Michigan. Frank Lloyd Wright one-storey studio-house, Oak Park, Illinois.

1904 Edwin H. Cheney house, 520 North East Avenue, Oak Park, Illinois. Robert M. Lamp house, 22 North Butler Street, Madison, Wisconsin. Larkin Company administration building, 680 Seneca Street, Buffalo, New York. Darwin D. Martin house, conservatory, garage, etc.; 125 Jewett Parkway, Buffalo, New York. *Projects:* Hiram Baldwin house, Kenilworth, Illinois. Robert D. Clarke house, Moss Avenue, Peoria, Illinois. Larkin Company workmen's rowhouse, Buffalo, New York. J. A. Scudder house, Campement d'Ours Island, Desbarats, Ontario, Canada. Frank L. Smith bank, Dwight, Illinois. H. J. Ullman house, North Euclid Avenue and Erie Street, Oak Park, Illinois.

1905 Mary M. W. Adams house, 103 Lake Avenue, Highland Park, Illinois. Hiram Baldwin house and garage, 205 Essex Road, Kenilworth, Illinois. Charles E. Brown house, 2420 Harrison Avenue, Evanston, Illinois. E-Z Polish factory for D. Darwin and W. E. Martin, 3005-3017 West Carroll Avenue, Chicago, Illinois. W. A. Glasner house, 850 Sheridan Road, Glencoe, Illinois. Thomas P. Hardy house, 1319 South Main Street, Racine, Wisconsin. W. R. Heath house, 76 Soldiers Place, Buffalo, New York. A. P. Johnson house, South Shore Road, Lake Delavan, Wisconsin. Lawrence Memorial library interior for Mrs. R. D. Lawrence, Springfield, Illinois. River Forest Tennis Club, Bonnie Brae Avenue and Quick Street, River Forest, Illinois. Rookery Building, remodelled La Salle and Adams Street entrance, lobbies and balcony in central court, La Salle and Adams Streets, Chicago, Illinois. Frank L. Smith bank, Dwight, Illinois. *Projects:* Charles W. Barnes house, McCook, Nebraska. T. E. Gulpin house, Kenilworth Avenue and North Boulevard, Oak Park, Illinois. Single-storey varnish factory. Hervey P. Sutton house, McCook, Nebraska. House on lake.

1906 P. A. Beachy house, 238 Forest Avenue, Oak Park, Illinois. K. C. de Rhodes house, 715 West Washington Street, South Bend, Indiana. Grace Fuller house, Hazel Avenue and Sheridan Road, Glencoe, Illinois. A. W. Gridley house and barn, North Batavia Avenue, Batavia, Illinois. P. D. Hoyot house, 318 South Fifth Avenue, Geneva, Illinois. George Madison Millard house, 410 Lake Avenue, Highland Park, Illinois. Frederick Nicholas house, Brassie Avenue, Flossmoor, Illinois. W. H. Pettit mortuary chapel, Belvedere cemetery, Belvedere, Illinois. River Forest Tennis Club, Lathrop Avenue, and Quick Street, River Forest, Illinois. C. Thaxter Shaw remodelled house, 3466 Peel Street, Montreal, Canada. Unity (Universalist) Church and Parish house, Kenilworth Avenue, at Lake Street, Oak Park, Illinois. *Projects:* Richard Bock studio house, Maywood Illinois. Devin house, Eliot, Mexico. 'A fireproof house for $5000', for the Curtis

Publishing Co. Walter Gerts (Alex Davidson) house, Glencoe, Illinois. R. S. Ludington house, Dwight, Illinois. Warren McArthur concrete apartment house, Kenwood, Chicago, Illinois. C. Thaxter Shaw house, Westmount, Montreal, Canada. Elizabeth Stone house, Glencoe, Illinois.

1907 George Blossom garage, 49th Street at Kenwood Avenue, Chicago, Illinois. E. W. Cummings Real Estate office, Harlem Avenue and Lake Street, River Forest, Illinois. Col. George Fabyan remodelled house, Batavia Road, south of Geneva, Illinois. Fox River Country Club remodelled for Col. George Fabyan, Geneva, Illinois. Stephen M. B. Hunt house, 345 South Seventh Avenue, La Grange, Illinois. Larkin Company pavilion, Jamestown Tercentenary exposition, Jamestown, Virginia. Emma Martin, alterations to Frick house and new garage, 540 Fair Oaks Avenue, Oak Park, Illinois. Pebbles and Balch decorating shop, 1107 Lake Street, Oak Park, Illinois. Andrew T. Porter house, Hillside, Spring Green, Wisconsin. Harvey P. Sutton house, 602 Main Street, McCook, Nebraska. F. F. Tomek house, 150 Nuttal Road, Riverside, Illinois. Burton J. Westcott house, 1340 East High Street, Springfield, Ohio. *Projects:* Harold McCormick house and adjuncts, Lake Forest, Illinois. Andrew T. Porter house, Hillside, Spring Green, Wisconsin.

1908 E. E. Boynton house, 16 East Boulevard, Rochester, New York. Browne's Bookstore, Fine Arts Building, 410 South Michigan Avenue, Chicago, Illinois. Avery Coonley house and stable, 300 Scottswood Road, Riverside, Illinois. Walter V. Davidson house and garage, 75 Tillingham Place, Buffalo, New York. Robert W. Evans house, 9914 Longwood Drive, Chicago, Illinois. E. A. Gilmore house, 120 Ely Place, Madison, Wisconsin. L. K. Horner house, 1331 Sherwin Avenue, Chicago, Illinois. Isabel Roberts house, 603 Edgewood Place, River Forest, Illinois. Dr G. C. Stockman house, 311 First Street, Mason City, Iowa. *Projects:* Frank J. Baker house, Wilmette, Illinois. E. D. Brigham stables. Dr W. H. Copeland remodelled house, 408 Forest Avenue, Oak Park, Illinois. William Norman Guthrie house, Sewanee, Tennessee. Horseshoe Inn for Willard H. Ashton, Estes Park, Colorado. Francis W. Little house, Wayzata, Minnesota. J. G. Melson house, Mason City, Iowa. Moving picture theater.

1909 Frank J. Baker house, 507 Lake Avenue, Wilmette, Illinois. City National Bank Building and Hotel for Blyth and Markley, West State Street and South Federal Avenue, Mason City, Iowa. Robert D. Clarke additions to little house and garage, 603 Moss Avenue, Peoria, Illinois. Dr W. H. Copeland alterations, 408 Forest Avenue, Oak Park, Illinois, Mrs Thomas H. Gale house, 6 Elizabeth Court, Oak Park, Illinois. J. Kibben Ingalls house, 562 Keystone Avenue, River Forest, Illinois. Meyer May house, 450 Madison Avenue S. E., Grand Rapids, Michigan. Frederick C. Robie house, 5757 Woodlawn Avenue, Chicago, Illinois. George C. Stewart house, 166 Hot Springs Road, Montecito, California. Peter C. Stohr building, shops, tearoom, etc., Wilson Avenue, Chicago, Illinois. W. Scott Thurber art gallery, Fine Arts Building, 410 South Michigan Avenue, Chicago, Illinois. *Projects:* Harry E. Brown house, Geneva, Illinois. Larwill house, Miskegon, Michigan. Lexington Terrace for Edward C. Waller Jr. and Oscar Friedman. Mrs Mary Roberts house, River Forest, Illinois. Edward C. Waller bathing pavilion, Charlevoix, Michigan. Edward C. Waller, small houses for rent, River Forest, Illinois. Town of Bitter Root for Bitter Root Irrigation Company, nr. Darby, Montgomery.

1910 J. H. Amberg house, 505 College Avenue, Grand Rapids, Michigan. E. P. Irving house, Millikin Place, Decatur, Illinois. Universal Portland Cement Co. exhibit, Madison Square Garden, Madison Square, New York. Rev. J. R. Ziegler house, 509 Shelby Street, Frankfort, Kentucky. *Project:* House and studio of Frank Lloyd Wright, viale Verdi, Fiesole, near Florence, Italy.

1911 Herbert C. Angster house, 650 Blodgett Road, Lake Bluff, Illinois. O. B. Balch house, 611 North Kenilworth Avenue, Oak Park, Illinois. Avery Coonley gardener's cottage, Scottswood Road, Riverside, Illinois. Taliesin I, Frank Lloyd Wright house, studio and farm buildings, Spring Green, Wisconsin. (1911–12) Banff National Park Pavilion, Canada. *Projects:* Harry S. Adams house, Oak Park, Illinois. Sherman M. Booth house, Glencoe, Illinois. Sherman M. Booth summer cottage. Avery Coonley greenhouse, Riverside, Illinois. Avery Coonley kindergarten, Riverside, Illinois. Arthur M. Cutten house, Downer's Grove, Illinois. E. Esbenshade house, Milwaukee, Wisconsin. Madison Hotel for Arthur L. Richards, Madison, Wisconsin. Andrew T. Porter house, Spring Green, Wisconsin. Edward Schroeder house, Milwaukee, Wisconsin. Frank Lloyd Wright house, Goethe Street, Chicago, Illinois.

1912 Avery Coonley playhouse, 350 Fairbanks Road, Riverside, Illinois. Lake Geneva Inn for Arthur L. Richards, Lake Geneva, Wisconsin. William B. Greene house, 1300 Garfield Avenue, Aurora, Illinois. Park Ridge Country Club addition and alterations, Park Ridge, Illinois. *Projects:* Kehl dance academy, residence and shops, Madison, Wisconsin. Schoolhouse, La Grange, Illinois. Press (San Francisco) Building for Spreckels Estate, Market Street, San Francisco. Taliesin cottages, Spring Green, Wisconsin.

1913 Harry S. Adams house, 710 Augusta Street, Oak Park, Illinois. Banff National Park recreation building, Banff, Canada. M. B. Hilly house, Brookfield, Illinois. Francis W. Little house, II, garage and boathouse, 'North-home', Wayzata, Minnesota. *Projects:* Art Museum. Carnegie Library, Pembroke, Ottawa, Canada. J. W. Kellogg house, Milwaukee, Wisconsin. Jerome Mendelson house, Albany.

1914 Midway Gardens for Edward C. Waller Jr and Oscar Friedman, Cottage Grove Avenue, at 60th Street, Chicago, Illinois. S. H. Mori oriental art studio, 801 Fine Arts Buildings, 410 South Michigan Avenue, Chicago, Illinois. Taliesin II, Frank Lloyd Wright house, Spring Green, Wisconsin. *Projects:* Honore J. Jaxon houses. State Bank, Spring Green, Wisconsin. United States Embassy, Tokyo. John Vogelsang dinner gardens and house, Chicago, Illinois.

1915 Emil Back house, 7415 Sheridan Road, Chicago, Illinois. Sherman M. Booth house, 265 Sylvan Road, Glencoe, Illinois. E. D. Brigham house, Sheridan Road, Glencoe, Illinois. A. D. German Warehouse, Richland Center, Wisconsin. Ravine Bluffs development for Sherman M. Booth, Glencoe, Illinois. *Projects:* American System Ready-Cut standardized houses and apartments for Richard Brothers, Milwaukee, Wisconsin. Chinese restaurant for Arthur L. Richards, Milwaukee, Wisconsin. Christian Catholic Church, Zion City, Illinois. Model Quarter Section development, Chicago, Illinois. Imperial Hotel, Tokyo. Rockefeller Foundation Chinese Hospital. Wood house, Decatur, Illinois.

1916 Joseph J. Bagley house, Lakeview and Cedar Avenues, Grand Beach, Michigan. F. C. Bogk house, 2420 North Terrace Avenue, Milwaukee, Wisconsin. W. S. Carr house, Lakeview and Pine Avenues, Grand Beach, Michigan. Imperial Hotel Annex, Tokyo. Arthur Munkwitz duplex apartments, 1102, 1104, 1110, 1112 North 27th Street, Milwaukee, Wisconsin. Arthur L. Richards houses, 1835 South Layton Boulevard and 2714 West Burnham Street, Milwaukee, Wisconsin. Arthur L. Richards duplex apartments, 2720, 2724, 2728, 2732 West Burnham Street, Milwaukee, Wisconsin. Ernest Vosburgh house, Crescent Road, Grand Beach, Michigan. *Projects:* Miss Behn (Voight) house, Grand Beach, Michigan. Clarence Converse house, Palisades Park, Michigan. William Allen White remodelled house, Emporia, Kansas.

1917 Henry J. Allen house, 255 Roosevelt Boulevard, Wichita, Kansas. Aizaku Hayhi house, Komazawa, Tokyo. Stephen M. B. Hunt house, 685 Algoma Avenue, Oshkosh, Wisconsin. Imperial Hotel, Tokyo. *Project:* Aline Barnsdall 'Hollyhock House', Theater, etc., Olive Hill, Los Angeles, California. Odawara Hotel, Nagoya, Japan. Powell House, Wichita, Kansas.

1918 Fukuhara house, Hakone, Japan. Yamamura house, Ashiya, Japan. *Projects:* Lord Immu House, Tokyo. Lord Inouye house, Tokyo. Moving picture theater, Tokyo.

1919 *Projects:* Monolith Homes development for Thomas P. Hardy, Racine, Wisconsin. W. S. Spaulding gallery for storage and exhibition of Japanese prints, Boston, Massachusetts.

1920 Aline Barnsdall House and garage, 'Hollyhock House', Sunset and Hollywood Boulevard, Edgemont Street and Vermont Avenue, Los Angeles, California. Aline Barnsdall studio residence, Hollywood Boulevard and Edgemont Street, Los Angeles, California. Aline Barnsdall studio residence B, 1645 Vermont Avenue, Los Angeles, California. W. J. Weber house, 9th Avenue at 4th Street. *Projects:* Aline Barnsdall theater, shops, apartments and houses to rent, Sunset Boulevard, between Edgemont Street and Vermont Avenue, Los Angeles, California. Cantilevered concrete skyscraper.

1921 Jiyu Gakuen Girls' School of the Free Spirit, Tokyo. Mrs Thomas H. Gale house or houses, Birch Brook, Whitehall, Michigan. *Projects:* Cement block house, Los Angeles, California. Edward H. Doheny ranch development, Sierra Madre mountains, near Los Angeles, California.

1922 *Projects:* A. M. Johnson desert compound and shrine, Death Valley, California. G. P. Lowes house, Eagle Rock, California. Merchandising building, Los Angeles, California. Sachse house, 'Deep Springs', Mojave Desert, California. Tahoe Summer Colony, Emerald Bay, Lake Tahoe, California.

1923 Aline Barnsdall kindergarten, 'The Little Dipper', Olive Hill, Los Angeles, California. Nathan G. Moore remodelled house, 329 Forest Avenue, Oak Park, Illinois. Dr John Storer house, 8161 Hollywood Boulevard, Los Angeles, California. Mrs George Madison Millard house, 645 Prospect Crescent, Pasadena, California. *Projects:* Darwin D. Martin house, for his daughter, Buffalo, New York. Hunting Lodge, Tahoe Summer Colony, Lake Tahoe, California.

1924 Charles Ennis house, 2607 Glendower Road, Los Angeles, California. Samuel Freeman house, 1962 Glencoe Way, Los Angeles, California. *Projects:* Nakoma Country Club and Winnebago Camping Ground Indian Memorial, Madison, Wisconsin. National Life Insurance Company skyscraper for A. M. Johnson, Water Tower Square, Chicago, Illinois.

1925 Taliesin III, Frank Lloyd Wright house, Spring Green, Wisconsin. *Projects:* Mrs Samuel William Gladney house, Fort Worth, Texas. Mrs George Madison Millard gallery, Pasadena, California. Phi Gamma Delta Fraternity House, Madison, Wisconsin. Gordon Strong Planetarium, Sugar Loaf Mountain, Maryland.

1926 *Projects:* Oak Park playground Association Playhouses, Oak Park, Illinois. Steel Cathedral embracing minor cathedrals to contain a million people, New York.

1927 Darwin D. Martin house and garage, 'Graycliff', Derby, New York. Ocotillo

Desert Camp. Frank Lloyd Wright Southwestern headquarters, Salt Range near Chandler, Arizona. *Projects:* Dr Alexander Chandler low-cost concrete block houses, Chandler, Arizona. Dr Alexander Chandler San Marcos-in-the-Desert winter resort, Chandler, Arizona. Wellington and Ralph Cudney house, San Marcos-in-the-Desert, Chandler, Arizona. Owen D. Young house, San Marcos-in-the-Desert, Chandler, Arizona.

1928 *Projects:* Darwin D. Martin Blue Sky mausoleum, Buffalo, New York. Standardized cillage service stations and city gasoline stations.

1929 Richard Lloyd Jones house, 'Westhope', 3700 Birmingham Road, Tulsa, Oklahoma. *Projects:* Richard Lloyd Jones house, Tulsa, Oklahoma. Elizabeth Noble apartment house, Los Angeles, California. Rosenwald Foundation school for Negroes. St. Mark's Tower for the Vestry of St. Mark's-in-the-Bouwerie, New York City, N.Y.

1930 *Projects:* Grouped apartment towers, Chicago, Illinois. Cabins for desert or woods.

1931 *Projects:* Capital Journal Building for George Putnam, Salem, Oregon. 'House on the Mesa', Denver, Colorado. Schemes for 'A Century of Progress', Chicago, Illinois.

1932 *Projects:* 'Conventional House'. Walter Davidson prefabricated sheet steel farm units. Walter Davidson prefabricated sheet steel and glass markets. New Theater. Dean Malcolm M. Willey house, Minneapolis, Minnesota.

1933 Taliesin Fellowship complex, Hillside, Spring Green, Wisconsin.

1934 Dean Malcolm M. Willey house, 255 Bedford Street, Minneapolis, Minnesota. *Projects:* Remodelling of A. D. German Warehouse as restaurant and apartments. Broadacre City (1934–58).

1935 *Project:* Stanley Marcus house, Dallas, Texas.

1936 S. C. Johnson Administration Building, 1525 Howe Street, Racine, Wisconsin. Edgar J. Kaufmann house, 'Falling Water', Bear Run, Pennsylvania. Mrs Abby Beecher Roberts house, 'Deertrack', R. F. D. Marquette, Michigan. *Projects:* H. C. Hoult house, Wichita, Kansas. Robert D. Lusk house, Huron, South Dakota

1937 Paul R. Hanna house, 737 Coronado Street, Palo Alto, California. Herbert Jacobs house, 441 Toepfer Street, Westmorland, near Madison, Wisconsin. Herbert F. Johnson Jr. house, 'Wingspread', Wind Point, north of Racine, Wisconsin. Edgar J. Kauffmann office, Kaufmann Department Store, 400 Fifth Avenue, Pittsburgh, Pennsylvania. *Projects:* 'All steel' houses development, Los Angeles, California. Leo Bramson dress-shop reconstruction, 1107 Lake Street, Oak Park, Illinois. George Parker garage, Janesville, Wisconsin.

1938 Ben Rebhuhn house, Myrtle Avenue and Magnolia Drive, Great Neck Estates, Great Neck, Long Island, N.Y. Taliesin farm group, Hillside, Spring Green, Wisconsin. Taliesin West, Frank Lloyd Wright winter headquarters in the desert, Maricopa Mesa, Paradise Valley, near Phoenix, Arizona. *Projects:* Edith Carlson house, Superior, Wisconsin. Florida Southern College, Lakeland, Florida. 'House for a family of $5000–$6000 income for *Life*. Ralph Jester House, Palos Verdes, California. Herbert F. Johnson Jr gatehouse and farm group, Wind Point, north of Racine, Wisconsin. Royal H. Jurgenson house, Evanston, Illinois. George Bliss McCullum house, Northampton, Massachusetts. E. A. Smith house, Piedmont Pines, California.

1939 Andrew F. H. Armstrong house, Ogden Dunes, near Gary, Indiana. Edgar J. Kaufmann guest house, Bear Run, Pennsylvania. Stanley Rosenbaum house, Riverview Drive, Florence, Alabama. Bernard Schwartz house, Still Bend, Two Rivers, Wisconsin. George D. Sturges house, 449 Skyway Road, Brentwood Heights, California. Tod Company 'Suntop Homes', quadruple house, Sutton Road at Spring Avenue, Ardmore, Pennsylvania. Katherine Winkler and Alma Goetsch house, Hulett Road, Okemos, Michigan. *Projects:* Lewis N. Bell house, Los Angeles, California. Madison Civic Center, Olin Terrace, Monona Avenue, Lago Monona, Madison, Wisconsin. Edgar A. Mauer house, Los Angeles, California. Ludd M. Spivey house, Fort Lauderdale, Florida. Usonian house development, Okemos, Michigan (for Winkler-Goetschn, Erling B. Brauner, J. J. Garrison, C. D. Hause, Sidney H. Newman, Alexis J. Panshin, E. Clerence, and R. Van Dusen).

1940 Theodore Baird house, Shays Street, Amherst, Massachusetts. Sidney Bazett house, 101 Reservoir Road, Hillsborough, California. James B. Christie house, Jockey Hollow Road, Bernardsville, New Jersey. Community Church, 4600 Main Street, Kansas City, Missouri. Joseph Euchtman house, Cross Country Boulevard by Labyrinth Road, Baltimore, Maryland. Florida Southern College, Ann Pfeiffer Chapel, Lakeland, Florida. Florida Southern College, seminar buildings, Lakeland, Florida. Lloyd Lewis house, Little St. Mary's Road, Libertyville, Illinois. Charles L. Manson house, 1224 Highland Boulevard, Wausau, Wisconsin. Rose Pauson house, Orange Road, Phoenix, Arizona. John C. Pew house, 3650 Mendoza Drive, Shorewood Hills, near Madison, Wisconsin. Loren Pope house, Locust Street, Falls Church, Virginia. Clarence W. Sondern house, 3600 Belleview

36 Frank Lloyd Wright in old age

Avenue, Kansas City, Missouri. Leigh Stevens house and adjuncts, Auldbrass Plantation, Yemassee, South Carolina. *Projects:* Crystal Heights hotel, theater, shops etc., Connecticut and Florida Avenue, Washington, D.C. John Nesbitt house, Cypress Point, Carmel Bay, California. Martin J. Pence house, Hilo, Hawaii. Frank A. Rentz house, Madison, Wisconsin. Franklin Watkins studio, Barnegat City, New Jersey.

1941 Gregor Affleck house, Bloomfield Hills, Michigan. Florida Southern College Library, Lakeland, Florida. Arch Oboler house, Ventura Boulevard, Los Angeles, California. John Barton house, Pine Bluff, Wisconsin. Alfred H. Ellinwood house, Deerfield, Illinois. Parker B. Field house, Airport Road, Peru, Illinois. William Guenther house, East Caldwell, New Jersey. Roy Petersen house, West Racine, Wisconsin. Stuart Richardson house, Livingston, New Jersey. Vigo Sundt house, Madison, Wisconsin. Carlton David Wall house, Detroit, Michigan. Mary Waterstreet Studio, near Spring Green, Wisconsin. *Projects:* Margaret Schevill house, Tucson, Arizona. Sigma Chi Fraternity House, Hanover, Indiana.

1942 *Project:* Co-operative Homestead.

1943 Chauncey Griggs house, 78 John Dower, Chambers Creek, Tacoma, Washington (1943–53).

1945 *Projects:* Elizabeth Arden Resort Hotel, 'Sunlight', Phoenix, Arizona. Arnold Friedman house, Pecos, New Mexico.

1946 Florida Southern College, Administration Building, Lakeland, Florida (1946–50). Erling Brauner house, Arrowhead, Road, Okemos, Michigan (1946–47). *Projects:* V. C. Morris house, San Francisco, California. Benjamin Adelman Laundry, Milwaukee, Wisconsin. Calico Mills Office Building, Attmedabad,

India. Rogers Lacy Hotel, Dallas, Texas.

1947 S. C. Johnson and Son, Administration Building and Research Tower, 1525 Howe Street, Racine, Wisconsin (1947–50). Arnold Friedman, Pecos National Forest, Pecos, New Mexico (1947–48). *Projects:* Huntington Hartford house, Hollywood Hills, California. Huntington Hartford Play Resort, Hollywood Hills, California. Self-Service Garage, Pittsburgh, Pennsylvania. Community Center, Point Park, Pittsburgh, Pennsylvania. Concrete 'Butterfly' Bridge, Wisconsin River, near Spring Green, Wisconsin. Ayn Rand House, Hollywood, California.

1948 Mrs W. C. Alpaugh house, Northport, Michigan (1948–49). Albert Adelman house, 7111 N. Barnett, Fox Point, Wisconsin. Herbert Jacobs house, Old Sank Road, Middleton, Wisconsin. V. C. Morris Shop, 140 Maiden Lane, San Francisco, California. Maynard Benhler, Great Oak Circle, Orinda, California. *Projects:* Warren Tremaine Observatory, Meteor Center, Meteor, Arizona. Nicholas P. Daphne Chapels, San Francisco, California.

1949 Lowell E. Walter house, Quasqueton, Iowa (1945–50).

1950 Isadore Einnerman house, Heather Street, Manchester, New Hampshire. Sol Friedman house, Usonia Homes, Pleasantville, New York. Ed Serlin house, Usonia Homes, Pleasantville, New York. J. A. Sweeton house, Kings Highway, Mercantville, New Jersey. Florida Southern College, Industrial Arts, Lakeland, Florida (1950–55). C. E. Weltzheimer house, Morgan Street, Oberlin, Ohio. Riverview Terrace Restaurant, under construction, Spring Green, Wisconsin. Raymond Carloson, 1123 W. Palo Verde Drive, Phoenix, Arizona. *Project:* A. K. Chahrondi house, Petra Island, Lake Mahojac, New York.

1951 Stuart Richardson house, Waldwick, New Jersey. Willis J. Hughes house 'Fountainhead', Jackson, Mississippi (1951–56). H. T. Mossberg house, 1405 Ridgedale Road, South Bend, Indiana. James Edwards house, Arrowhead Road, Okemos, Michigan. Melwyn Maxwell Smith house, 50045 Pon Valley Road, Blomfeld Hills, Michigan. William Palmer house, 227 Orchard Hills Drive, Ann Arbor, Michigan. David Weisblatt house, 11185 Hawthorn Drive, Galesbury Village, near Kalamazoo, Michigan. Curtis Meyer house, 11108 Hawthorne Drive, Galesbury Village, near Kalamazoo, Michigan. Eric Pratt house, 11036 Hawthorn Drive, Galesbury Village, near Kalamazoo, Michigan. Ward Greiner house, 2617 Taliesin Drive, Kalamazoo (Parkwyn Village), Michigan. Eric. V. Brown house, 2806 Taliesin Drive, Kalamazoo (Parkwyn Village), Michigan. Robert Levin house, 2816 Taliesin Drive, Kalamazoo Parkwyn Village, Michigan. Robert D. Winn house, 2822 Taliesin Drive, Kalamazoo, Parkwyn Village, Michigan. Howard Anthony house, 1150 The Army Road, Benton Harbor, Michigan. Ina Morris Harper house, Lake Shore Road, St Joseph, Michigan. Richard Smith house, 801 Lindar Street, Jefferson, Wisconsin. Uniterian Meeting house, 900 University Bay Drive, Madison, Wisconsin. Kenneth Laurent house, Spring Brook Road, Rockford, Illinois. John C. Carr house, 1544 Portago Run, Glenview, Illinois. Henry J. Neils house, 12815 Burnham Boulevard, Minneapolis, Minnesota. Dr A. H. Bulbulian house, Skyway Drive, Rochester, Minnesota. Thomas E. Kzyzs house, Skyway Drive, Rochester, Minnesota. S. P. Elam house, 107 Eastwood Road, Austin, Minnesota. Dr L. A. Miller house, 701 E. Blount Street, Charles City, Iowa. Douglas Grant house, Carroll Drive and Adal Street, Cedar Rapids, Iowa. Carrol Alsop house, 1907 A Avenue E, Oskaloosa, Iowa. Jack Lamberson house, 117 N. Park Oskaloosa, Iowa.

1952 A. K. Chahroudi house, Petra Island, Lake Mahojac, New York. Louis Marden house, 4413 Chainbridge Road, McLean, Virginia. Florida Southern College, Science Building, Lakeland, Florida. Seamur Shavin house, 334 N. Crest Road, Chattanooga, Tennessee. Patrick Lancaster House, Wisconsin (1952–53). Robert Muirhead house, south west of Village Plato Center, Illinois. David Wright house, Paradise Valley, Arizona. Robert Berger house, 259 Redwood Road, San Anselmo, California (1952–59). Arthur Matthews house, Wisteria Way, Lindenwood Estates, Atherton, California. Mrs Clinton Walker house, Scenic Drive, Carmel, California.

1953 W. L. Fuller house, Paso Christian, Mississippi. Nathan Rubin house, 518 44th Street, N. W. Canton, Ohio. Samuel Eppstein house, 11098 Hawthorne Drive, Galesburg Village, Michigan. Russel M. Kraus house, 120 N. Ballas Road, Kirkwood, Missouri. Price Tower, Bartlesville, Oklahoma (1953–56). Jorgine Boomer house, 5804 N. 30th Street, Phoenix, Arizona. Benjamin Adelman house, 5710 N. 30th Street, Phoenix, Arizona. Quentin Blair house, Cody, Wyoming. Anderton Court Center, Rodeo Drive, Beverly Hills, Los Angeles, California (1953–54). Joseph H. Brewer house. 'Rhododendron' Chapel, Bear Run, Connellsville, Pennsylvania. Point View Apartment Tower, Pittsburgh, Pennsylvania. *Projects:* Masieri Memorial, Venice, Italy. Trinity Chapel, Norman, Oklahoma.

1954 Ronald Reisley house, Usonia Homes, Pleasantville, New York. Maximilian Hoffman house, North Manursing Island, Rye, New York. I. N. Hagan house, Chalk Hill, Ohiopyle Road, Uniontown, Pennsylvania. Dr Richard Davis house, Shady Hills, Marion, Indiana. Donald Loveness house, Route 3, Woodpile Lake, Stillwater.

1955 Frank S. Sander house, Springbough, Woodchuck Road, Stamford, Connecticut. Mercedes-Benz Show Room, 430 Park Avenue, New York City. R. L. Wright house, 7929 Deepwell Road, Bethesda, Maryland. Florida Southern College, Danforth Chapel, Lakeland, Florida. Karl A. Staley house, Lake Road, Madison, Ohio. Louis Penfield house, River Road, Willoughby, Ohio. J. Dobkins house, 5120 Plain Canter Road, Canton, Ohio. Ellas A. Fieman house, 452 Santa Clara Drive, N.W., Canton, Ohio. Lewis H. Goddard house, 12221 Beck Road, Plymouth, Michigan. Ward McCartney house, 2662 Taliesin Drive, Kalamazoo (Parkwyn Village), Michigan. Dr Maurice Greenburg house, Highway 67, Dousman, Wisconsin. Clark Arnold house, 954 Line Road, Columbus, Wisconsin. Charles F. Glore house, 170 North Mayflower, Lake Forest, Illinois. R. W. Lindholm house, Cloquet, Minnesota. W. L. Thaxton Jr. house, 12024 Tall Oaks, Houston, Texas. Archie Boyd Teater Hageman Valley, Bliss, Idaho. Dr Karl Kundert Medical Building, 1106 Pacific Street, San Louis, Obispo, California. *Projects:* Lenkurt Electric Company Building, Long Island, New York. Daniel Wieland Motor Hotel, Hagerstown, Maryland.

1956 John L. Rayward house, Frogtow Road, New Canaan, Connecticut (1956–58). Guggenheim Museum, 5th Avenue and E. 88th Street, New York City (1956–59). Abraham Wilson house, Main Street, Millstone, New Jersey. Beth Sholom Synagogue, Old York Road, Ilkins Park, near Philadelphia, Pennsylvania (1956–59). Dudley Spencer house, 619 Shipley Road, Wilmington, Delaware. Cedric Boulter house, 1 Rawson Wood Circle, Cincinnati, Ohio. Annunciation Greek Orthodox Church, N. 92nd Street and W. Congress Streets, Wauwatosa, Wisconsin. Willard H. Keland house, Valley View Drive, Racine, Wisconsin. Harold C. Price, Jr Country Club Terrace, Bartlesville, Oklahoma. Harold C. Price Jr house, Paradise Valley, Arizona. W. B. Tracy house, 1897 Edgecliff Drive, Seattle, Washington. *Project:* Skyscraper 'The Golden Beacon', Chicago, Illinois.

1957 Toufic H. Kalil house, Heather Street, Manchester, New Hampshire. Duey Wright house, Highway 51, Wausau, Wisconsin. Arnold Jackson house, Beltline Avenue, Madison, Wisconsin (1957–58). Erdman Company, First Pre-Fab, Rosa Road, near Crestwood, Madison, Wisconsin. Wyoming Valley School, Route 23, Wyoming Valley, Wisconsin. Lewis B. Frederick house, County Line Road, Barrington, Illinois (1957–58). First Pre-Fab, Donlea Road, Barrington, Illinois (1957–58). Lindholm Filling Station, Cloquet, Minnesota (1957–58). John Gillin house, 9400 Rockbrook, Dallas, Texas (1957–58). *Projects:* Plan for Greater Baghdad; Opera House and Garden; University Complex and Gardens, Baghdad, Iraq. Wedding Chapel, Claremont Hotel, Berkeley, California. Arizona State Capital, 'Oasis', Phoenix, Arizona.

1958 Andrew B. Cooke house, 403 Crescent and 41st Street, Virginia Beach, Virginia (1958–59). Dr Kenneth Meyer Clinic, Dayton, Ohio. (1958–59). William Boswell house, Cincinnati, Ohio (1958–59). George Dlesk house, Manistee, Michigan. Stanley Harman house, Lansing, Michigan (1958–59). Donald Schoberg house, 1155 Wrightwind Drive, Okemos, Michigan. Oscar Miller house, Milford Village, Okemos, Michigan (1958–59). Dorothy Turkel house, 2760 W. Seven Mile Road, Detroit, Michigan. Carl Schultz house, Benton Harbor, Michigan (1958–59). First Pre-Fab, Stevens Point, Wisconsin. First Pre-Fab, Joseph Malaca, Builder, Bayside, Wisconsin. Robert Sunday house, Marshalltown, Iowa (1958–59). Paul Trier house, Des Moines, Iowa (1958–59).

1959 First Pre-Fab, Staten Island, New York. Florida Southern College, Music Building, Lakeland, Florida. Erdman Company, Second Pre-Fab, Madison, Wisconsin. Kalita Humphrey's Theater, Dallas, Texas. *Project:* Manhattan Sports Pavilion, New York City.

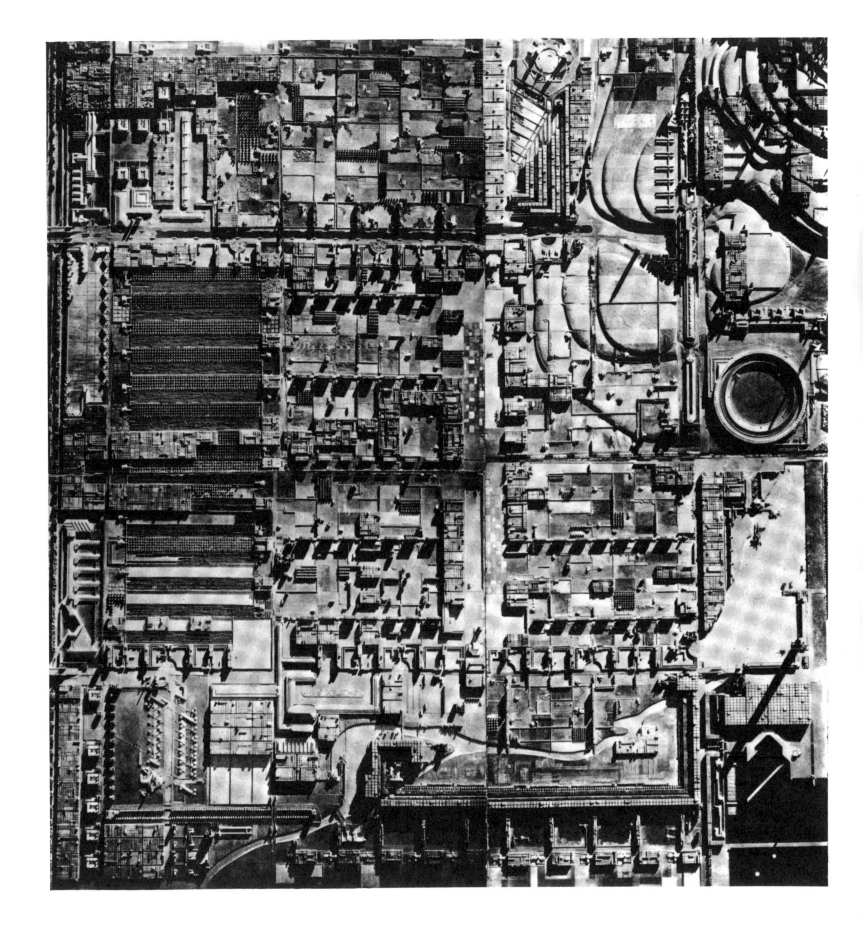

37 Model of Broadacre City

Bibliography

WRITINGS OF FRANK LLOYD WRIGHT

The Art and Craft of the Machine, Chicago, 1901. XIV. Exhibition of Chicago Architectural Club (catalogue); *In the Cause of Architecture*, in 'Architectural records', March 1908; *Frank Lloyd Wright, Ausgeführte Bauten und Entwürfe*, Wasmuth, Berlin, 1910 (preface in German): *The Japanese Print: an Interpretation;* Ralph Fletcher Seymour, Chicago, 1912; *In the Cause of Architecture,* 'Architectural Records', May 1914; *The New Imperial Hotel* and *In the Wake of the Quake I and II,* in 'Western Architect', April and November 1923, and February 1924; *Louis Henry Sullivan, Beloved Master,* in 'Western Architect', June 1924; *Louis Sullivan, His Work,* in 'The Architectural Records', July 1924; *In the Cause of Architecture: The Third Dimension,* in the volume on his work mentioned in the bibliography published at Santpoort, Holland, in 1925; *In the Cause of Architecture (I The Architect and the Machine, II Standardisation, III the Soul of the Machine, IV Steel Fabrication and Integration: The New World),* in 'The Architectural Record', May, June, July, August and September 1927; *The Frank Lloyd Wright collection of Japanese Prints,* catalogue for the auction sale, Anderson Galleries, New York, January 1927; *I In the Cause of Architecture, II The Logic of the Plan, III Styles' Mean to the Architect, IV The Meaning of Materials: Stone, V The Meaning of Materials: Wood, VI The Meaning of Materials: The Kiln, VII The Meaning of Materials: Glass, VIII The Meaning of Materials: Concrete, IX The Meaning of Materials: Sheet Metal, X The Terms),* in 'The Architectural Record', January, February, April, May, June, July, August, October, December 1928; *Modern Architecture. The Kahn Lectures for 1930,* Princeton Monographs in Art and Archeology, Princeton 1931; *Two Lectures on Architecture,* The Art Institute of Chicago, 1931; *An Autobiography,* Duell, Sloan and Pearce, New York, 1931; Faber and Faber, London, 1946; *The Disappearing City,* New York, 1932; *The Taliesin Fellowship,* Spring Green, Wisconsin, 1932; *Taliesin,* Spring Green, Wisconsin, 1934; *Broadacre City: A New Community Plan,* in 'The Architectural Record', April 1936; *Recollections: United States 1893–20,* in 'The Architects Journal', London, July–August 1936; *Architecture and Modern Life* (in collaboration with B. Brownell), Harper, New York, 1937; *Architecture and Life in the U.S.S.R.,* in 'The Architectural Record', October 1937; *A New House by Frank Lloyd Wright on Bear Run, Pennsylvania* (Preface), The Museum of Modern Art, New York, 1938; *An Organic Architecture: The Architecture of Democracy* (Lecture at the Royal Institute of British Architects), Lund Humphries, London, 1939; *Chicago's Auditorium; is Fifty Years Old,* in 'The Architectural Forum', September 1940; *Frank Lloyd Wright on Architecture, selected writings, 1894–1940* (edited by Frederick Gutheim), Grosset and Dunlop, New York, 1941; *When Democracy Builds,* University of Chicago Press, Chicago, 1945; *Genius and the Mobocracy,* Duell, Sloan and Pearce, New York, 1949; *Building for Modern Men. A Symposium edited by Thomas A. Creighton,* New Jersey, 1949; *Organic Architecture Looks at Modern Architecture,* in 'The Architectural Record', May 1952; *The Future of Architecture,* Horizon Press, New York, 1953; *The Natural House,* Horizon Press, New York, 1954; *The Story of the Tower,* New York, 1956; *A Testament,* Horizon Press, New York, 1957; *The Living City,* New York, 1958; *Frank Lloyd Wright: Writings and Buildings,* selected by Edgar Kaufmann and Ben Roeburn, Meridian Books, New York, 1960; *The Solomon R. Guggenheim Museum,* The Solomon R. Guggenheim Foundation and Horizon Press, New York, 1960.

WRITINGS ON FRANK LLOYD WRIGHT

ROBERT C. SPENCER J., *The Work of Frank Lloyd Wright,* in 'The Architectural Review', June 1900; *Frank Lloyd Wright, a Village Bank,* in 'Brickbuilder', August 1901; *The Work of Frank Lloyd Wright; his influence,* in 'The Architectural Record', July 1905; RUSSEL STURGIS, *The Larkin Building, Buffalo, N.Y.,* in 'The Architectural Record' XXII, March 1908; THOMAS E. TALLMADGE, *The Chicago School,* in 'The Architectural Review', April 1908; *Ausgeführte Bauten und Entwürfe von Frank Lloyd Wright* (with a preface by Wright) Wasmuth, Berlin, 1910; *Frank Lloyd Wright: Ausgeführte Bauten* (with a preface by C. R. Ashbee), Wasmuth, Berlin, 1911; MONTGOMERY SCHNYLER, *An Architectural Pioneer; Review of the portfolios containing the works of Frank Lloyd Wright,* in 'The Architectural Record', April 1912; HENDRICK P. BERLAGE, Amerikaanse Reisherinneringen, Rotterdam, 1913; ALFRED B. YLOMANS, *City Residential land development studies in planning,* Chicago, c. 1916; HENDRIK BERLAGE, *Frank Lloyd Wright,* Wendingen, Santpoort, 1924; HENRICUS THEODOR WIJDEVELD, *The life and work of the American Architect Frank Lloyd Wright,* C. A. Mees, Santpoort (Holland), 1925; RICHARD NEUTRA, *Eine Bauweise in bewehrtem Beton an Neubauten von Frank Lloyd Wright,* in 'Die Baugilde', February 1925; LEWIS MUMFORD, *The Life Work of the American Architect, Frank Lloyd Wright,* Mees, Santpoort (Holland), 1925 (published in seven numbers of 'Wendingen'); HERMAN SOERGEL, *Wright, Dudok Mendlesohn,* München, 1926; JACOBUS P. OUD, *Holländische Architektur,* Stuttgart, 1927; RICHARD NEUTRA, *Wie Baut Amerika?,* Stuttgart, 1927; HENRY RUSSEL HITCHCOCK JR., *Frank Lloyd Wright* 'Maîtres de l'Architecture Moderne' series, n. 1), Paris, 1928; F. KIMBALL, *American Architecture,* New York, 1928; S. LAFOLLETTE, *Art in America,* New York, 1929; HENRY RUSSEL HITCHCOCK, *Modern Architecture; Romanticism and Reintegration,* New York, 1929; RICHARD NEUTRA, *Amerika, Die Stilbildung des Neuen Bauens in den Vereinigten Staaten,* Schroll, Vienna, 1930; G. PLATZ, *Die Baukunst der neusten Zeit,* Berlin, 1930; HENRY RUSSEL HITCHCOCK, *Frank Lloyd Wright, International Exhibition, Museum of Modern Art,* in 'Modern Architecture', New York, 1932; *Early Modern Architecture: Chicago 1870–1910,* The Museum of Modern Art, New York, 1933 (and 1940); THOMAS CRAVEN, *Modern Art,* Simon and Schuster, New York, 1934; P. HORTON SHAND, *Scenario for a Human Drama,* in 'The Architectural Review', London, February 1935; THOMAS TALLMADGE, *The Story of Architecture in America,* Norton, New York, 1936; WALTER C. VELIRENDT, *Modern Building,* Harcourt, Brace, New York, 1936; TALLOT A. HAMLIN, *Frank Lloyd Wright,* in 'Pencil Points', 1938; LEWIS MUMFORD, *The Culture of Cities,* New York, 1938; *A New House by Frank Lloyd Wright on Bear Run, Pennsylvania,* The Museum of Modern Art, New York, 1938; SIGFRIED GIEDION, *Space, Time and Architecture,* Harvard Press, Cambridge, Mass., 1941; HENRY RUSSEL HITCHCOCK, *On the Nature of Materials. The Buildings of Frank Lloyd Wright 1887–41,* Duell Sloan and Pearce, New York, 1942; ELIZABETH MOCK (Editor), *Built in U.S.A., 1932–1944,* The Museum of Modern Art, New York, 1944; JOHN LL. WRIGHT, *Our Father Who is on Earth,* New York, 1946; MIES VAN DER ROHE, *A Tribute to Wright,* in 'College Art Journal', 1946; WILLIAM SENER RUSH, *Frank Lloyd Wright,* in Thieme-Becker, Künstlerlexicon, Vol. XXXVI, 1947; BRUNO ZEVI, *Towards an Organic Architecture,* Faber and Faber, London, 1949; NICHOLAS PEVSNER, *Pioneers of Modern Design from William Morris to Walter Gropius,* Museum of Modern Art, New York, 1949; BRUNO ZEVI, *Frank Lloyd Wright and the Conquest of Space,* in 'Magazine of Art', Vol. 43, n. 5, Washington D.C., May 1950; E. KAUFMANN JR, *Taliesin Drawings: Recent Architecture of Frank Lloyd Wright selected from his drawings,* New York, 1952; WERNER M. MOSER (editor), *Sechzig Jahre Lebendige Architektur (Sixty Years of Living Architecture); Frank Lloyd Wright,* Winterthur Zürich, 1952; HENRY RUSSEL HITCHCOCK, A. DREXLER, *Built in U.S.A.: Postwar Architecture,* The Museum of Modern Art, New York, 1952; HENRY RUSSEL HITCHCOCK, *The Evolution of Wright, Mies and Le Corbusier,* in 'Perspecta', n. I, 1952; LEWIS MUMFORD, *Roots of Contemporary American Architecture,* New York, 1952; *Drawings by Frank Lloyd Wright,* in 'Architectural Record', May 1952; *Wright,* Solomon R. Guggenheim Museum, November 1953; V. SCULLY, *Wright versus the International Style,* in 'Art News', n. 1, 1954; E. KAUFMANN, *An American Architecture, Frank Lloyd Wright,* New York, 1955; B. KARPEL, *What Men have written about Frank Lloyd Wright,* in 'House Beautiful Magazine', November 1955; VINCENT SCULLY, *The Shingle Style; Architectural theory and design from Richardson to the origins of Wright,* Yale, 1955; *Guggenheim Museum to rise–victory for Wright in twelve-year design battle,* in 'Architectural Forum', June 1956; G. C. MANSON, *The First Golden Age, Frank Lloyd Wright 1910,* New York, 1958; PETER BLAKE, *Frank Lloyd Wright: Master of Architectural Space,* in 'Architectural Forum', September 1958; E. KAUFMANN, *Form of Space for Art; Wright's Guggenheim Museum,* in 'Art in America', winter 1958–59; R. LYNES, *Mr. Wright's Museum,* in 'Harper's Magazine', November 1959; *Wright's Starling Museum Spiral,* in 'Life', 2 November 1959; B. KAUFMANN, *Wright's Museum,* in 'Commonwealth', 4 December 1959; LEWIS MUMFORD, *Skyline,* in 'The New Yorker', 5 December 1959; PETER BLAKE, *The Guggenheim: Museum or Monument?,* in 'Architectural Forum', December 1959; H. KRAMER, *Month in Review: New Guggenheim Museum,* in 'Arts', December 1959; M. D. SCHWATZ, *New Solomon R. Guggenheim Museum,* in 'Apollo', December 1959; A. FORSEE, *Frank Lloyd Wright, Rebel in Concrete,* Philadelphia, 1959; G. FERRAZ, *Posicão de F. Ll. Wright,* in 'Habitat', n. 53, 1959; E. KAUFMANN, *Frank Lloyd Wright, Drawings for a living architecture,* New York, 1959; JOHN CANADAY, *Wright vs. painting scores design.* in 'New York Times', 21 October 1959; R. M. COATES, *Art Galleries,* in 'New Yorker', 31 October 1959; VINCENT SCULLY, *Frank Lloyd Wright,* New York, 1960; *Frank Lloyd Wright: The Solomon R. Guggenheim Museum,* The Solomon R. Guggenheim Foundation and Horizon Press, New York, 1960; OLGIVANNA LLOYD WRIGHT, *The Shining Brown,* New York, 1960; PETER BLAKE, *The Master Builders,* London, 1960; F. GUTHEIM, *Wright Legacy evaluated,* in 'Architectural Review', October 1960; M. SCHUYLER, *American Architecture and Other Writings,* Cambridge, March 1961; J. BURCHARD, A. BUSH-BROWN, *The Architecture of America: A social and cultural history,* Boston, 1961; J. MARTSON FITCH, *Architecture and the aesthetics of plenty,* New York, 1961; JOVANNA LLOYD WRIGHT, *Architecture, Profession of the Earth,* New York, 1962; A. DREXLER, *The Drawings of Frank Lloyd Wright,* New York, 1962; F. FARR, *Frank Lloyd Wright,* London, 1962; HENRY RUSSEL HITCHCOCK, V. SCULLY, A. BROOKS, J. SUMMERSON, *The XX International Congress of the history of Art,* Princeton, 1963; C. W. CONDIT, *The Chicago School of Architecture,* Chicago-London, 1964; A. SIEGEL (editor), *Chicago's Famous Buildings,* Chicago-London, 1965; *The Work of Frank Lloyd Wright,* Horizon Press, New York, 1965 (with a preface by Olgivanna Lloyd Wright); H. JACOBS, *Frank Lloyd Wright: America's greatest architect,* New York, 1965; J. M. DENNIS, L. B. WENNEKER, *Ornamentation and the Organic Architecture of Frank Lloyd Wright,* in 'Art Journal', autumn 1965; OLGIVANNA LLOYD WRIGHT, *Frank Lloyd Wright, his Life, his Work, his Words,* New York, 1966; N. KELLY SMITH, *Frank Lloyd Wright: a study in architectural content,* Englewood Cliffs, 1966; RAYNER BANHAM, *Frank Lloyd Wright, as environmentalist,* in 'Architectural Design', vol. XXXVII, n. 4, 1967: E. KAUFMANN, *Frank Lloyd Wright: the eleventh decade,* in 'Architectural Forum', June 1969.